SOCIAL INTELLIGENCE AND GENDER

C. MARGARET HALL

Social Intelligence and Gender *is a guide to discovering the power and complexities of gender and social influences, as well as the impacts they have on our freedom and opportunities. This book is dedicated to readers who want to better themselves, their accomplishments, and the world we live in.*

Table of Contents

Social Intelligence Sheds Light on Gender

Social Intelligence Guides Gender

Social Intelligence Expresses Gender

Social Intelligence
Sheds Light on Gender

I. Social Intelligence Today

Social intelligence is a relatively modern discovery in social sciences. At the same time that social scientists applied concepts such as self and role to understanding human behavior, they began to realize that individual-focused personality theories do not adequately describe or explain why repeated patterns of behavior permeate our families, beliefs, social classes, cultures, and societies. However, when we search for a fuller understanding of familiar patterns of behavior, we see that the power and complexities of major social influences often predispose us to have particular attitudes toward ourselves, others, and the world, and that these same social influences frequently compel us to act in specific ways whether we want to do so or not.

Scrutinizing our observations and experiences are dependable ways to become aware of our social intelligence. This information shows us that all human beings have some significant others, with the result that we often acknowledge their impacts on us whenever we assess our social situations and options. For example, we are usually raised in the social contexts of families, and move among varied social spheres continuously throughout our lifetimes. In these respects, we are inevitably beholden to whichever major social influences impact us the most.

We are born with social intelligence, which includes our capacities to understand and deal with wide ranges of social influences. At best we continue to use our social intelligence to guide us throughout our lives—either deliberately or intuitively—so that we are able to navigate our day-by-day social situations effectively. Consequently, we can also decide whether or not to increase our social intelligence in our negotiations with others, especially in accomplishing particular goals. When we are socially intelligent, we ultimately accept more serious responsibilities, such as contributing to the common good or social justice. In so doing, using social intelligence increases the possibility that we benefit our societies as well as ourselves. For example, when we set out to make the world a better place for all, we necessarily improve our life satisfaction, as well as contribute to others in worthwhile ways.

We increase our social intelligence by examining how our current social intelligence developed or was conditioned until the present. For example, we begin to see and learn how our experiences in families, beliefs, social classes, cultures, and societies predispose us to have particular views of self and others. Furthermore, when we use the broad perspectives of social intelligence to think about ourselves in relation to families, beliefs, social classes, cultures, and societies, we are more objective and more critical of how and what we need to change in order to increase our impacts on everyday situations. We examine carefully the growth of our social intelligence through our families, beliefs, social classes, cultures, and societies, because these strong social influences have emotional pulls on our loyalties, especially through the attitudes and values we developed as children or young adults.

The tasks involved in exploring who we are in our families, beliefs, social classes, cultures, and societies are enormous, difficult, and challenging. For example, we easily get down-hearted when looking at who we are shocks or horrifies us. Consequently, we may decide not to pursue such a discomforting venture. However, the complexities of our identities and behavior can be unsnarled to some extent, and deliberately increasing our social intelligence gives us more control over our lives. Because social intelligence prevents us from dissipating our energies, we become more efficient, as well as more effective, when we sort out what our preferred goals are, and how to accomplish them more directly.

Importantly, our capacities to be socially intelligent deepen our understanding of our genders—the ways in which we have been socialized to be men or women—as well as our sexualities and sexual orientations. Whatever the physiology of our genders, sexualities, and sexual orientations, we can change some of what many people consider to be limiting characteristics, through applying social intelligence principles to our goals and objectives. For example, our gender and sexuality choices are strongly influenced by how much social intelligence we choose to nurture and use.

Social intelligence helps us to change given characteristics of our individual and social situations as well as who we are. For example, we are who we are not only because of our personal inclinations,but because of how we interact with those who are the most emotionally significant to us. In addition, we are integral parts of constantly changing patterns of exchanges in broad social influences such as history, globalization, and evolution.

Gender Defined

Gender is more ambiguously defined today than in previous decades, although slow changes in gender definitions have developed steadily throughout the last few centuries. A meaningful measure of contrasting gender definitions results from comparing genders in the last three generations of our families. For example, we see that some contrasts between past and present definitions of gender include new emphases on similarities between men and women, sometimes including similarities between men and women with different sexual orientations. Even though women and men may continue to be thought of as social classes in their own right, choosing the cultural value of equality now reflects some of the deepest interests held by both women and men in contemporary societies.

In many respects today people consider genders to be learned behavior, rather than behavior dictated by biological differences. For example, populations are sufficiently aware of the impacts of social and cultural influences, that we generally believe that gender is learned—and therefore possible to change—during our lifetimes. Although some gender changes may be relatively insignificant in the total scheme of things, marked shifts in gender behavior may help us to adapt to the stresses that we necessarily face daily as modern adults.

Changing our initial gender conditioning calls into question our original gender definitions. For example, making deliberate gender changes in response to historical exigencies, such as war, often makes populations less polarized in their assumptions about men's and women's characteristics. As a result we now see men and women not as people who have traditional roles to play, but rather as unique individuals, who often have more contrasting agendas and behavior differences among men and among women, than between men and women.

However we decide to define our genders, we need to accept the fact that our gender identities are strong components of how we think about ourselves, others, and the world. For example, we often identify with women or men with similar genders, so that we develop a more detailed understanding and appreciation for those who have genders like our own. Moreover, because we recognize our tendencies to identify with people of the same gender, we understand more fully the depth of gender conditioning in our families when we were young.

For these reasons we need to take our gender identities seriously. For example, paying attention to how we define our genders helps us to avoid becoming entrapped by our gender identities. Furthermore, to the extent that we view and understand that our genders are fluid, ever-changing but significant identities, we increase our options as well as our social intelligence.

Being socially intelligent today requires us to sort out how our genders are influenced by our families, beliefs, social classes, cultures, and societies in both the past and the present. We discover, for example, that our social worlds are in perpetual motion, and that we need to make some sense out of the varied pressures of the major social influences of families, beliefs, social classes, cultures, and societies on our genders, if we are to survive and live fully in our complex modern societies. In these respects, self-definitions of gender may sometimes be insufficient, because we need to respond continuously to how others see and define us. Although we usually cannot control the social definitions others bestow on our genders, deliberately choosing how we define our genders will make us more effective in achieving our individual and social goals.

Social intelligence is a means to an end. We use our social intelligence to assess our starting points, for example, so that we can map out more accurately how to accomplish the objectives we set for ourselves. Social intelligence also gives us the means to assess our ongoing trajectories in everyday life, so that we do not allow our genders to interrupt or diminish how we increase the common good and social justice.

When we use social intelligence to explore our own changing definitions of genders, we first focus on how we were raised as boys or girls, and how we are as men or women. We try to discern which gender assumptions guided our parents, siblings, and grandparents when we were young, for example, because these same influences frequently persist throughout our lifetimes as repeated patterns of behavior or powerful social expectations. Thus, social intelligence sheds light on how we developed the genders we have, so that we can take more advantage of new options to change our behavior as women and men.

Gender and Sexuality

Because public opinion often distorts our understanding of both genders and sexualities, often by assuming some kind of direct connection or symmetry between biological sex and gender conditioning, it is more realistic to consider human behavior as in part influenced by biological drives, and in part a product of social influences. For example, we are usually born either male or female genetically—regardless of significant shades of difference in these sexual polar opposites—and we are then raised or encouraged to be either male or female, depending on social or emotional conditions in our families and cultures.

For the purpose of thinking about genders more fully, through using social intelligence as described in *Social Intelligence and*

Gender, we consider genders and sexualities as related but different. For example, sexualities in *Social Intelligence and Gender* refer to our universal biological or genetic heritages, as well as to the different sexual orientations and world views of members of the same and opposite sexes. Thus, in spite of the social fact that most women and men have contrasting physiological characteristics and world views, genders emphasize socialized orientations as females or males rather than their differences in sexualities.

The above distinctions are overly simplistic, but can inspire useful working definitions of ourselves and the world, particularly through social intelligence, genders, and sexualities. Succeeding chapters in *Social Intelligence and Gender* discuss basic concerns about genders and sexualities, as well as the central importance of social intelligence in making choices about genders and sexualities. For instance, we may be exactly what the world expects of us in relation to genders and sexualities, or we may choose not to conform to others' expectations. Differences between genders and sexualities frequently evoke ambivalence for us and our significant others, with the result that social intelligence usefully guides us to make new decisions about how we want to be in the world.

In these respects, *Social Intelligence and Gender* clarifies important issues about genders and sexualities, and shows us how being socially intelligent about our sexual identities helps us to deal with the negative reactions that others may have toward our sexualities and genders. Because social intelligence helps us to live more fully, we are ultimately more satisfied in our everyday lives. For example, social intelligence guides us to make the most of our gender conditioning, and also allows us to be true to ourselves in relation to the strong social influences of families, beliefs, social classes, cultures, and societies.

We may find that trying to separate our genders from our sexualities and sexual orientations, in order to be more closely guided by social intelligence, is virtually impossible. However, from the point of view of social intelligence, both gender and sexuality are meaningful distinctions to make in spite of the difficulties in doing so. For example, we gain objectivity about ourselves by separating gender from sexuality. This increases our freedom to think more clearly about our options and daily decision-making, even if we focus more on our genders than on our sexualities and sexual orientations, or vice versa. Moreover, giving close attention to our genders helps us to resolve some of the stresses and pressures we experience from our sexualities and sexual orientations.

Social intelligence suggests that the five major social influences affect the depth and impact of our social conditioning. For example, when we want to understand our genders more fully in relation to our sexualities, we need to see what our gender conditioning was and is in our families, beliefs, social classes, cultures, and societies. In fact, only by assessing our genders in these significant social spheres do we get more in charge of our ongoing gender conditioning. These particular five social influences are at the core of social intelligence, and are individually and socially significant, because they consistently exert strong emotional pressures on our deepest loyalties and affections. Our genders, sexualities, and sexual orientations not only have deep-seated cultural ties, but they also galvanize some of our deepest desires and emotions.

Applying broad socially intelligent perspectives to our genders, such as considering life outcomes, inspires us to increase our social intelligence. Social intelligence teaches us that our genders and sexualities are not fixed by our biological and genetic heritages, but are malleable to some extent, particularly in how we deal with the givens of our biological and genetic heritages. For example, when we realize that our gender conditioning relates directly to our families, beliefs, social classes, cultures, and societies, we can decide to change some of the impacts of our families' influences by making new value choices.

Gender and Sexual Orientation

Social intelligence helps us to be more aware of our sexual orientations as well as our genders. When we examine our sexualities, we realize that our sexual orientations have more

7

biological foundations than the gender conditioning we receive through our families and other social influences. However, for the purpose of allowing social intelligence to guide our expressions of both our genders and our sexual orientations, it is often useful to consider gender and sexual orientation as separate facets of our being and behavior. Furthermore, cultivating a degree of detachment from these major aspects of our identities increases our objectivity and options in making decisions that affect us and others.

Our growing awareness of our genders and sexual orientations shows us that gender and sexual orientation are dominant and complex influences in our lives, whether we consider biological aspects of gender in sexual orientations, or social influences on our genders and sexual orientations. Given these important complexities, social intelligence is a reliable guide for understanding and acting in varied social situations.

Social intelligence claims that social aspects of genders and sexual orientations have continuing impacts on our behavior, whether we realize this or not. Consequently, it is worthwhile to make as many deliberate choices as possible in deciding which aspects of our genders and sexual orientations we want to maintain, develop, or change. The power of social intelligence in these processes does not mean that social intelligence changes genetic or physiological characteristics of our sexual orientations, but rather that social intelligence helps us to decide what it is about our biological sexual orientations that we want to express privately or socially.

We often construct or maintain our gender identities without necessarily being aware of our sexual orientations, especially if we are heterosexual rather than homosexual. For example, we may naively believe that sexual orientation applies to other people rather than to ourselves, if we habitually express the dominant sexual orientation of our societies. When we have a heterosexual orientation, we often consider ourselves as "normal" or "natural," while those with a homosexual orientation may be thought of as "deviant" or even "evil," rather than merely "different."

I. Social Intelligence Today

Social intelligence helps us to reduce both our positive and negative emotional reactivity—which may include stultifying ambivalence, anxiety, or fear—usually toward those who have different sexual orientations from us. Although our gendered responses to heterosexual or homosexual orientations vary according to dominant patterns in our genders, other social influences are also involved. For example our families, beliefs, social classes, cultures, and societies play crucial roles in helping us to understand the intensity of our reactions to both sexual orientations and gender issues.

The reason why we cannot ignore sexuality and sexual orientation, in trying to understand our genders, is that these are integral aspects of our genders without being all that genders are. Although our sexualities and sexual orientations may be more clearly defined by biology than environmental conditions, some social influences do affect our sexuality and sexual orientations deeply. In these respects, social intelligence helps us to live more productively, and with a greater degree of individual and social fulfillment, in relation to our genders, sexualities, and sexual orientations.

From the point of view of the passage of time, we have more social awareness about our genders, sexualities, and sexual orientations today than we would have had in earlier historical times. Similarly, we are more knowledgeable today about how our emotions govern our genders, sexualities, and sexual orientations in both the past and the present. For example, evolution is widely accepted as slow, gradual changes whereby we become increasingly in control of our earliest fight or flight emotional foundations of human behavior and civilizations. Similarly, even though recorded histories may not yield much evidence of real progress in the development of the human spirit, some of the most egregious excesses of human behavior have been somewhat curtailed by modern legal systems.

Social intelligence today—our capacities to understand and act responsibly in relation to the major social influences of families, beliefs, social classes, cultures, and societies—sheds much light

9

on gender and sexuality issues that ruled much of our decision-making in the past. For example, we are freer men and women today than in ancient times, because of the relatively reliable knowledge base of social intelligence. Our socially intelligent know-how about the impacts of the five major social influences of families, beliefs, social classes, cultures, and societies guides us to find meaningful ways to express our genders and sexualities, so that we build just societies for more people, as well as move toward constructive futures.

Gender Choices

Social intelligence today shows us that there are many more gender choices in the present than a hundred years or even a generation ago. These additional choices result in part from our heightened awareness and increased social experiences of varied gender options as children, adolescents, young adults, mature adults, and elders. Some gender choices also result from the sexualization of modern societies, largely due to increased consumerism, new industrial technologies, and commercialization.

Present-day education and current public opinion challenge traditional thinking that suggests that we are responsible when we meet others' expectations by playing roles that have been repeated through the generations. For example, in the past individuals and populations took for granted that they were obligated to follow in the footsteps of same-sex parents and grandparents. In these respects, gender choices were severely limited by cultural attitudes and available opportunities, especially with regard to most women and some men.

Social intelligence helps us to be aware of historical changes in gender expectations, so that we become more objective in our understanding of the possibilities and restrictions of our gender options. When we are more realistic about our starting points in gender choices, for example, we are more likely to create new opportunities for ourselves, rather than merely duplicate the gender roles of those who lived before us.

I. Social Intelligence Today

Another important aspect of our heightened awareness of social intelligence and gender patterns is that we benefit from thinking of ourselves as individuals rather than gender categories. For example, there is so much variation among individuals that we are clearly not going to be able to realize our opportunities, as women or men, if we consider only conventional gender options when we assess our choices and opportunities today. Rather, we must live responsibly and sufficiently deeply as individuals, so that we are both willing and able to forge new gender and sexual destinies for ourselves in the present and the future.

Social intelligence is a tool that helps us to be considerably more knowledgeable about today's gender situations, as well as enables us to be more discriminating in our everyday gender choices. Whereas traditions, religions, and cultures often present limited gender choices that reflect the past, commercial images of consumerism offer new ways that both increase and restrict our present gender freedoms. By contrast, social intelligence requires us to see and understand the extent to which we live according to the domination of particular social and gender influences, so that we are more able to seize our freedom in the present, and build meaningful lives in the future for ourselves and others.

According to social intelligence, many of our gender choices of the past and present are understood by scrutinizing gender options in our families, beliefs, social classes, cultures, and societies. Social intelligence is based on social facts that reflect and represent these five major social influences, because they often impact the extent to which we are tied to unrealistic expectations for expressing gender and sexual aspects of our lives. An effective, socially intelligent strategy, which increases flexibility in our gender choices, is to trace some of the gender and sexual limitations we express in the varied social spheres of our families, beliefs, social classes, cultures, and societies. This makes us more effective in avoiding the relentlessness of these patterns in the present and the future.

Therefore, increasing our social intelligence allows us to live more fully. We take the social issue of gender sufficiently seriously, so that we increase our gender options and those of our children and others. For example, we take center stage in our own lives more decisively, when we recognize the many ways in which gender inequalities permeate our choices today. Consequently, we become more astute in making new gender choices in the present for the future.

Social intelligence holds out great promise for actively choosing our genders, sexualities, and sexual orientations. Although as human beings we do not usually select our genetic or physiological characteristics, we can choose how to be who we are, as well as how to define and live our genders, sexualities, and sexual orientations each day. Whatever we learn can be unlearned, and in this respect social intelligence opens doors for us that are as yet unimagined.

Gender choices become more central to our existential social quests to survive and be fulfilled, because we learn that we must make new gender choices deliberately in order to live fully. We cannot survive or be fulfilled in the long run, unless we increase the historical or traditional gender choices available in all conventional social contexts today. We do not do this to increase disputes or competition between women and men, but rather to meet our shared needs to be who we are, as well as to build improved future societies.

Gender Responsibilities

Social intelligence is a readily available means we can choose to become more responsible in our actions. For example, when we understand the dominant social influences in our lives—families, beliefs, social classes, cultures, and societies—we make more effective socially intelligent decisions, and pursue socially intelligent goals which benefit others as well as ourselves. Social intelligence helps us to understand how families, beliefs, social classes, cultures, and societies influence our genders, and how we learn from assessing these influences on our genders.

Social intelligence enhances our awareness about our gender responsibilities in our daily decisions and goals. This benefit occurs because when we are more interested in the advantages of social intelligence, we see ourselves and our lives differently from merely going with the flow of our social conditioning. For example, when we deliberately work at increasing our social intelligence, we care more about whether our decisions and actions are responsible, and we face up to significant existential issues such as doing what we prefer most in our everyday lives.

Being more aware of the influences of families, beliefs, social classes, cultures, and societies on our genders and life outcomes, makes us question what we routinely take for granted about our gender responsibilities. Such questioning is constructive, because it helps us to check whether our gender assumptions are reliable guides for our decisions, commitments, and actions. For example, once we gain objectivity about our genders, we are ultimately more responsible in whatever we choose to do.

Thus, social intelligence gives us means to assess whether we are reaching our preferred goals successfully or responsibly, and guides us to make any changes needed to become more effective and responsible. For example, when our know-how is socially intelligent, we predict the consequences of our chosen actions more accurately, so that our efforts have more long-lasting impacts.

Although to some extent women and men appear to have different responsibilities according to their genders, there are significant common denominators of concern about responsibilities which apply to both women and men. For example, we are responsible for becoming and being the best possible women or men that we can be, so that we accomplish our preferred goals for others as well as ourselves. Ultimately, social intelligence supports quests for our collective fulfillment, rather than solely individual or collective survival, because when we accomplish some of our optimal goals all gain satisfaction and fulfillment from our contributions.

By contrast, when we are overly gender-specific in pursuing our goals, we necessarily short-change our social intelligence and inevitably repeat traditional gender stereotypes, rather than reach for gender identities which reflect and respond constructively to vital changed social situations in our modern societies. For example, we cannot be responsible if we use partial views of social realities, rather than full pictures of who we are and what we want to accomplish.

Our major shared gender responsibilities may often include representing the needs and wishes of those who find it difficult to articulate what they need or want. Identifying with people who have similar gender concerns, sexualities, or sexual orientations is an effective socially intelligent way to represent our deepest interests. This also requires us to be bold in assuming responsibilities that meet the needs of significant others as well as ourselves.

Our gender responsibilities must stay rooted in the present. Although we may only understand gender inequalities fully when we look directly at the past, our attention is sharpened by urgency when we consider gender responsibilities in the present for the future. We find our most constructive gender goals when we use our energies responsibly in the present: we aim to create responsible gender innovations rather than reinforce traditional gender expectations. We build more constructive and more egalitarian societies responsibly, when we respond positively to existential challenges in the present.

Social intelligence does not require us to take responsible actions when we first learn about social intelligence. Initially, we need to strengthen the foundations of our social intelligence by aiming to contribute to the common good and social justice. When we begin to consider our genders more thoughtfully, we gradually make more responsible contributions to the common good and social justice. Therefore, we become responsible historical actors slowly, by trying to solve issues related to gender in the present for the future.

Gender Fulfillment

Social intelligence is necessarily rooted in past and present social conditions, and at the same time moves us toward constructive futures. However, even though social intelligence is informed by the past, in many ways the past reflects directions that we do not choose to take now, or ways in which populations have produced unnecessary inequalities and alienation. We need to assess our present circumstances accurately in the present, if we are to take current opportunities to build futures that promise and deliver increased gender satisfaction for all.

Gender fulfillment often overlaps with individual and social fulfillment. Just as we want to live our lives purposefully as socially intelligent human beings, we also want to express our genders meaningfully as socially intelligent people. Although social intelligence shows us that the past has sometimes been made up of exploitative and oppressive gendered behavior, social intelligence also suggests that even though we inevitably learned some destructive gendered ways of being and doing, we can conduct ourselves differently in the present for the future.

In many ways, social intelligence today is more a promise of future gender fulfillment than a transformation of existing gender conditions. For example, we often find deficiencies in gender fulfillment for both women and men in modern societies, even though present trends in gender fulfillment may seem to contrast markedly from the severe gender injustices of past or contemporary traditional societies. Furthermore, there is no critical mass working for the gender fulfillment of women in their everyday life in most societies.

When we ask the significant socially intelligent question of how we can have gender fulfillment in the present for the future, we conclude that we must go in directions which increase our social intelligence. That is, we first examine the major social influences that restrict us the most, due to their frequently negative emotional impacts on our actions. For example, we try to discover patterns in social trends in our families, beliefs, social classes, cultures, and societies that encourage us to repeat unproductive individual and collective behavior through the generations, so that we can change our gendered reactions whenever possible.

Because each new generation in societies has to learn afresh about how to relate to each other, communities, societies, and the world, we can only promise and produce gender fulfillment when we develop constructive ways to think and act in the present. Sometimes this is achieved by increasing our social intelligence, by contributing decisively to the common good, or by making commitments to strengthen social justice. For example, when we make these new value choices in modern societies, we increase innovative ways to foster equality, inclusiveness, diversity, cooperation, and openness that gradually make gender fulfillment possible.

Social intelligence is governed by how we deal with our genders privately and publicly. It is insufficient to seek merely personal resolutions of gender conflicts, however, because whatever we do in our personal lives is strongly impacted by broad social trends in families, beliefs, social classes, cultures, and societies. We must be sufficiently aware of the interpersonal, local, national, and global dimensions of social conditions in our lives, if we are to rise up and represent not only our own self-interests, but also the needs of members of less powerful groups.

In order to change our levels of gender fulfillment, we examine to what extent we are currently fulfilled—or not—in our families, beliefs, social classes, cultures, and societies. This working knowledge makes us more objective in creating social conditions that increase gender fulfillment through equality, inclusiveness, diversity, cooperation, and openness. Optimally, we do this at the same time that we work with significant others to accomplish constructive universal goals.

Although we are most effective when we cooperate with likeminded others to establish social conditions for gender fulfillment, this intention does not necessarily involve working with people of the same gender. Rather, we may work more productively with those who want to express and fulfill their different genders in similar ways. Even though we necessarily share some interests with same sex gender groups, our understanding also varies according to social influences such as social classes or sexual orientations. For example, same sex gender groups of men or women may differ according to the age of the men and women who strive to increase gender fulfillment.

I. Social Intelligence Today

Trying to become more socially intelligent often creates better-coordinated working groups to accomplish gender fulfillment goals. However, it is difficult to identify groups of people who are sufficiently focused on gender fulfillment to address the most essential social issues that would increase meaningful gender identities or commitments. For example, it may be only when individuals work together on explicit social justice issues that they are sufficiently motivated to establish equality, inclusiveness, diversity, cooperation, and openness in their everyday gendered lives and beyond.

II. Families and Gender

Another way to see how social intelligence sheds light on our understanding of gender, and the impacts of gender on our lives, is to examine the five major social influences that most strongly affect who we are: families, beliefs, social classes, cultures, and societies. When we recognize linkages between these five major social influences and how we think, act, react, and interact, we can move further toward accomplishing our preferred goals.

In many respects, social intelligence guides us to formulate and express our chosen goals. By contrast, our genders frequently prevent us from accomplishing what we value most. For example, social intelligence helps us to size up our present situations, as well as to understand how our genders frequently deceive us in making sense of our worlds. Consequently, we become freer and more effective when we express who we really are, and what we truly want to accomplish, through cultivating and deliberately using our social intelligence.

The most powerful social influence that impacts our social intelligence is our families. Families are strong emotional bonds that permeate deep levels of our being when we are young, and continue to wield power over how we think and behave in many varied social settings. Because we are usually raised in our own or others' families, our most established patterns of social interactions derive mainly from these particularly significant emotional systems. We are who we are largely because of patterns of dependence and independence in our nuclear families and extended kin groups, in past as well as in present generations.

We become more socially intelligent, as well as more aware of our initial gender conditioning, when we examine how we developed some of our most basic emotional attitudes in our families. For example, our tendencies to be active or passive may be affected by our genders to some extent, especially by what went on in our families when we were very young. However, because these distinctive patterns of behavior—to be consistently active or passive—frequently govern all our lifetime commitments, we cannot afford to accept them merely as integral aspects of our genders.

More importantly, we benefit from looking toward our families to describe and explain who we are and what we do, as well as to shed light on the strength of our motives to bring about real changes in our personal and social situations. Moreover, because the emotional sources of our being derive from our families, we can only come to terms with these positive and negative influences when we use social intelligence to examine patterns of dependence in our families that were present when we were young, and which persist as powerful emotional influences in the present.

The strong emotional reactivity of our families predispose us to absorb particular patterns of gendered behavior. These repeated exchanges become diverse foundations for how we mature as women and men, through interacting with our relatives and others. For example, the power of gender identification in our families—our tendencies to identify with female relatives if we are girls, or with male relatives if we are boys—is particularly powerful due to families' emotional intensity. Consequently, much of our adult behavior may unwittingly repeat relatives' ways of coping with gender pressures.

Social intelligence helps us to come to terms with the power of emotional dependencies in our families, so that we do not merely succumb to extending or repeating our family emotional dependencies in other social settings or future generations. For example, when we deliberately strengthen our social intelligence, we become more objective about our value choices. Furthermore, social intelligence guides us, so that we no longer need to essentially duplicate gendered patterns of family behavior, which have been passed down through several generations of our families. Thus, social intelligence makes us more immune to the power of emotional dependencies in our families, as well as to conventional or stereotypical patterns of behavior associated with our genders.

In these and other ways, social intelligence increases our options in relation to our genders, sexualities, and sexual orientations. For example, when we conform to pressures in our families' emotional systems, we are inclined either to repeat or rebel against gendered expectations in our families. By contrast, when we are socially intelligent, we are more objective about our gender choices. Social intelligence helps us to distinguish gender choices which further our quests to live meaningfully, to contribute to the common good, and to increase social justice rather than make automatic, thoughtless gender choices that diminish our lives.

Gender Defined

In many respects our families define our genders during critical developmental stages of our lives. We are quickly labeled as male or female after our births—usually without ambiguity—and from this point on male or female cultures are instilled in us as significant social realities in our everyday lives. Furthermore, as children we cannot generally ignore the power of our gender socialization, nor can we ignore other important aspects of our ongoing socialization. Therefore, our points of departure, in the earliest years of our lives, are our physiological genders, as well as those gender cultures into which we were born.

Because we are dependent on our families at least until young adulthood, defining our genders is inextricably tied to how our families see us, in addition to how we see ourselves. For example, if we have sexual orientations which are different from the heterosexual majorities in our societies, we may not be accepted as "normal" boys or girls in our families—a rejection which is sometimes prolonged for a lifetime.

Another social reality, related to our families' vested interests in defining our genders, is that our families may try to maintain particular standards of behavior around our genders as we grow to maturity. For example, it is increasingly difficult for children and adolescents to resist the polarization of values that accompanies the assumptions of worth made by families about being male or female. Because of gender polarizations, other variations in orientation among boys and men, or girls and women, tend to be overlooked. For example, it may be too difficult for families to accept gendered behavior that seems to threaten traditional, conventional dichotomies through unusual gender contrasts.

This baseline of family experiences, where some of the strongest emotions of parents, grandparents, and children are invested in children's gendered upbringing, frequently results in both genders being defined oppressively. Social intelligence encourages us to see that we are who we are because of the strong, clear-cut gender definitions in our families, and that this is why the power of families' gender orientations is frequently experienced as irreversible or restrictive. Furthermore, our deep-seated quests to be human show us that we are more complex, with respect to our genders, than these powerful dualistic family pressures suggest.

Social intelligence demonstrates that an essential part of our struggle for survival and fulfillment is our need to enlarge the most limiting characteristics of our families' gender conditioning. For example, examining our gender socialization leads us to conduct ourselves as individuals—as selves—rather than to endlessly accept strong family pressures to conform to relatives' expectations for particular gender roles or gendered behavior. Thus, social intelligence helps us to transform our negative reactions to our limited freedom into socially valuable behavior, which gradually expands the common good and social justice.

In so doing, social intelligence guides us to develop empathy, because it requires us to wrestle with family pressures that unnecessarily restrict our lives. Social intelligence also shows us that we should not resist assuming responsibilities for others by turning inward to be self-serving in our interests and objectives. For example, when having fun supersedes our stated preferences to formulate constructive goals for ourselves and others, we make altruism impossible, and eventually reduce meaning and fulfillment in our everyday lives.

II. Families and Gender

At best, social intelligence broadens our perspectives on ourselves, our communities, and our societies, so that we become more objective about choosing what we can do. Moreover, when we habitually refer to the broader pictures of our lives, we gain the moral fortitude necessary to resist relatives' pressures to be who they expect us to be. At the same time, we become more independent and selective in our value choices about our genders. For example, social intelligence shows us that we have strong responsibilities to develop our genders as we want, because gender is at the core of our being and our contributions to the world.

However, social intelligence also shows us that gender is not the totality of our being. Although we are our genders, and we use our genders in order to live fully, we must develop goals that orient us to others in diverse ways. For example, we resolve to interact deliberately with our communities and societies, rather than solely with our families or other small groups. In so doing, we recognize that a significant part of maturity and independence means doing whatever we can to make the world a better place, rather than exploiting the world's resources for self-centered ends.

Gender and Sexuality

Sexuality continues to be a taboo topic in many families. In spite of improved education, which includes sex education from young ages, many sexual overtones of gender issues are not discussed or examined in families' everyday lives. Consequently, genders and sexualities are often not associated with each other in families' imaginations. For example, gendered disciplines tend to be seen as essential to family order and well-being, whereas sexualities are more often thought of as highly personal decisions that need not necessarily have family or social consequences.

Social intelligence heightens our awareness about genders, and at the same time links genders to physiological sources of sexualities and sexual orientations. Social intelligence raises existential questions, such as whether we can afford to lose sight of the significance of our sexual physiologies, for example, when many complex social influences pressure us to conform to diverse aspects of gender in our daily activities. Rather, social intelligence alerts us to the fact that we must be constantly aware of exploitative and oppressive aspects of sexualities and sexual orientations, so that we can enlarge and live according to our most constructive re-definitions of our genders.

Much of our resistance to focusing on our sexualities derives from how our families viewed and lived with sexualities across different generations. For instance, when families are too embarrassed to discuss sexualities, their lack of family openness predictably inhibits the sexual and social freedom of members of the youngest generations as they approach adulthood. By contrast, when families are both comfortable and thoughtful in discussing sexualities in past and current generations, their children develop more mature attitudes to sexualities, and consequently understand more fully how their sexualities are linked to their genders.

Social intelligence shows us that many of the behavioral nuances we associate with genders are essentially protections that control the physiological needs of particular individuals, communities, and societies. As human beings we procreate to perpetuate the human race, and social intelligence brings this need to the forefront of our attention when we continue to examine the social dynamics of genders and sexualities. For example, to the extent that we emphasize physiological differences between men and women in our gender expectations, we may merely be considering—mistakenly—that nature alone will meet all our complex physiological and survival needs.

However, our families do require us to control our sexualities, so that we honor economic and cultural resources that have been accumulated by elders or deceased members of past generations. For example, social intelligence reminds us that even though physiology may underpin social hierarchies of members' possessions, as well as gender differences and sexual attractiveness, we need to consider other complex qualities of family resources. For example, physiological concerns about sexualities and sexual orientations are ultimately tied to value choices as well as to procreation issues—that is, they are intense and volatile issues in families' emotional systems and societies.

Social intelligence teaches us to respect the biological characteristics of sexualities and procreation, without surrendering our whole lives to shared basic needs for physiological procreation. Although we may consider that our sexuality and bringing children into the world are vital to our happiness, the broad perspectives of social intelligence require us to formulate many goals that are not necessarily directly related to genders or physiologies. For example, our scrutiny of the five major social influences of families, beliefs, social classes, cultures, and societies shows us that common good and social justice goals should be addressed, which may at the same time seem remote from gender and sexuality survival concerns.

Given our complex physiological and social needs, families and societies usually control genders and sexualities through different aspects of the social institutions of marriage. For example, we learn, as children, that we are expected to create our own families and have children when we are adults, and that eventually we may be responsible for meeting our parents' physiological needs. However, this relatively closed cycle of stages in families' development lacks the true breadth of perspectives and outreach that social intelligence brings to bear on our everyday lives.

Although the social controls of marriage may be effective for regulating the everyday genders and sexualities of family members, this institutional need is frequently inadequate to inspire meaningful lives that aim to contribute to the common good and increase social justice. Social intelligence shows us that we must necessarily broaden our perspectives, by realizing that we have responsibilities to those outside our families who are less fortunate than we are, or who cannot help themselves. Furthermore, we need socially intelligent broad views of social realities, in order to live more meaningfully with zest and interest.

Gender and Sexual Orientation

In order to understand families' emotional systems, as well as the different roles that family members play in their emotional systems, social intelligence shows us that it is essential to consider at least three generations of family members, so that we can recognize repeated patterns in their dependencies. In these respects, individual family members participate in large kin groups, rather than merely in small nuclear families of parents and children, even though emphases on nuclear families still dominate conventional thinking about families in modern societies.

From the broad perspectives of social intelligence, individual members of current kin groups often have sexual orientations that resemble the sexual orientations of past and present members of the same kin groups. However, when some relatives in the same kin groups have different sexual orientations from the majority of their members, pressure to conform is frequently brought to bear on them.

When we use social intelligence to understand the interactions of kin group members, we find that kin members frequently conform rigidly to the sexual orientations of most members of their societies. Because this majority pattern of heterosexual orientation is duplicated and reinforced in most nuclear families, kin groups, communities, and societies, it is usually extremely difficult for individual family members with homosexual or other sexual orientations to live comfortably in their families and societies. For example, when having homosexual orientations is viewed as threatening the status quo of the more widely shared heterosexuality, families frequently bring strong pressures to bear on individual family members who do not conform to heterosexual standards of behavior.

The emotional climate produced by deliberately or automatically reinforcing social pressures, which aim to coerce family members to conform to heterosexual orientations, ultimately discriminate strongly against family members with homosexual orientations. Consequently, homosexual family members continuously risk being misunderstood, being uncomfortable, or being thought of as unproductive. If our preferred sexual orientation is homosexual, it is difficult to stand up against strong heterosexual majorities for our individual family rights, even though we may realize intellectually that we are entitled to do so. From the points of view of social intelligence, however, claiming our rights to be equal as individuals is beneficial for us, our kin groups, communities, and societies in the long run.

Social intelligence helps us to see the power and complexities of heterosexual inclinations, and at the same time supports efforts of individuals who try to be true to their homosexual orientations. This means that just as we need to choose how to express our genders and sexualities, we also need to choose how to express our sexual orientations, whatever they are. Social intelligence confirms that we are all equally responsible, whatever our genders, sexualities, and sexual orientations may be.

Social intelligence also requires us to consider our lives in relation to whole societies and globalization, as well as in relation to our families and communities. We learn that in order to live fully we must put our genders, sexualities, and sexual orientations at the center of how we think and act. Social intelligence requires us to be responsible by formulating constructive goals that contribute to the common good and social justice. This means that although genders, sexualities, and sexual orientations are very significant aspects of what we do on a daily basis, they do not require all our attention all of the time. Existentially, we need to make commitments to meet particular shared needs that include but go beyond our genders, sexual identities, and sexual orientations.

Because sexual orientations that are different from the majority of members of populations often need to be managed more carefully than mainstream heterosexuality—for example, with regard to marriages or long-term partnerships—deeper commitments are required to claim individual and societal rights to share social privileges appropriately when we are homosexual. Furthermore, because societies need contributions to the common good and social justice to improve the status of homosexual individuals and communities, homosexual people may consistently make more value choices than others to honor equality, inclusiveness, diversity, cooperation, and openness.

When we aim to build better societies for the future, we benefit from deciding to use our genders, sexualities, and sexual orientations as motivations to improve social conditions for future generations as well as ourselves. For example, we become more effective advocates for freer sexual orientations by being responsible historical actors, because this helps us to secure more sexual orientation rights for more members of our kin groups, local communities, societies, and the world.

Gender Choices

Social intelligence makes us aware of our current gender choices, as well as able to make new gender choices. Because social intelligence guides us to understand our gender socialization more deeply—by examining how we developed our genders through our families, beliefs, social classes, cultures, and societies—we begin to realize that we can change gender choices we have made in the past, as well as embrace different gender choices in the present for the future.

Thus, social intelligence enlightens our gender choices, and shows us how to express our genders constructively, so that we increase gender choices for others as well as us. Carving out such freedom in our gender choices is significant, because when we increase our own gender choices, we are more effective in securing similar freedoms for others. Furthermore, democracies benefit from nurturing this increased freedom, so that the quality of life in international communities gradually improves.

Although we do not make full gender choices as children, because our existence and survival are too often dependent on conforming to our parents' gender standards, we are socially intelligent as children. The choices we make when our dependency needs are strongest usually help us to survive, for example, and form foundations of patterned choices which we can change at any time, especially when we have sufficient emotional will and stamina to follow our preferences.

II. Families and Gender

We are all socially intelligent to some degree, or we could not survive in our societies today. The challenge of being socially intelligent is to continue to work at reorganizing the power that the five major social influences of families, beliefs, social classes, cultures, and societies have over us, so that we can make more deliberate choices each day about these strong influences. For example, we must avoid making automatic choices, because these usually reflect others' pressures to conform, rather than express our preferences to work on our most constructive goals.

Gender choices affect gender issues or broad social problems about the common good and social justice. When we focus on continuing to cultivate social intelligence, for example, we necessarily meet both gender and social needs. Although gender is an important aspect of general well-being, which permeates everything we do, we need to relate to others as equals whatever their genders, sexualities, and sexual orientations.

In order to establish social conditions for gender and sexual equality in societies, we must address shared survival and fulfillment needs. However, because gender inequalities often result from sexual oppression and sexual exploitation, we need to consider power relations in our communities and societies, as well as in our families, in order to build firm foundations for socially just families and societies. For example, social intelligence helps us to consolidate social facts, so that we are more effective in implementing constructive family and social strategies to achieve gender equality.

We can go so far as to say that social intelligence is largely about making choices, which includes making gender choices. We claim freedom as human beings not only because of political ideologies such as democracy, but as individuals and societies who must co-exist peacefully. We are responsible for the worlds we create, and this responsibility results in part from our gender choices.

When we concentrate on our gender choices, we prepare ourselves to be historical actors who opt to change social conditions in societies. We address the personal needs of our families by making particular choices, for example, and at the same time reach out to societies with common good goals and strategies. Our gender choices guide us at all times, because we are gendered beings who need to show compassion for others as well as ourselves.

When we consider our gender identities from the points of view of genders, sexualities, and sexual orientations, we find rich arrays of choices that may have been hidden from view for much of our lives. Our greatest gift to ourselves and others is to ponder these many choices as we go about our daily activities, and to give these same choices to members of the youngest generations of our families. Passing on the main messages of social intelligence in these ways is both fulfilling and rewarding, because it lays foundations for stronger families and more open societies in the present and future.

Gender Responsibilities

Social intelligence calls us to discover and deliver everyday responsibilities. Although it may be comforting to vote for strong leaders in democracies, we are still responsible for how we live our own lives, the sense we make of our worlds, and the goals we put into action. Therefore, we develop our social intelligence to guide us in these endeavors, so that we express our best selves more effectively through our value choices and enlightened actions.

Because gender is a significant source of our emotions and energies, we have to decide how to define and identify with our genders, as well as what we want to accomplish because of our genders, sexualities, and sexual orientations. In these respects, our genders are resources and talents, and our social intelligence guides us to be productive in bringing about changes in our lives and our families' experiences.

Unfortunately, this kind of socially intelligent thinking often does not make sense to many of us initially. However, alternatives to being socially intelligent in our gendered decisions frequently have destructive consequences, such as making mistaken assumptions about gender by acting automatically. For example, although we may comfort ourselves by imagining that it is meaningful to make our decisions and commitments intuitively, without examining our motives and the results of our actions for our families and others in the long run, we would be mistaken.

Being responsible for our genders is primarily being aware of our motives and the results of our actions. This means that we do not behave differently without scrutinizing why we use particular strategies, and how well our actions bring forth the results that we want. Social intelligence heightens our awareness of our know-how about the consequences of our actions, so that we become more responsible for whatever we do as we increase our social intelligence—especially when we apply social intelligence to our everyday lives rather than merely to a few strategies or social situations.

When we are aware of our gender responsibilities with regard to our families, beliefs, social classes, cultures, and societies, we fine-tune our motives and capacities to meet our preferred goals. Being socially intelligent about our gender responsibilities requires us to compare our motives and the results of our actions with the social facts of our situations, so that we make commitments to change who we are and what we do if we fall short of who we want to be and what we want to accomplish. In these respects, social intelligence helps us to become more responsible for our genders, sexualities, and sexual orientations in our families and other social contexts.

For example, we may decide that it is responsible to come out of the closet about our homosexuality, even though this decision may seem disruptive. Or, we may consider it wiser and more responsible to be deliberately subtle and discriminating about how we express our sexualities in our social relations. Social intelligence does not clearly indicate which actions we should take, but rather guides us in how we understand our actions in our exchanges with others. Therefore, our gender responsibilities frequently depend on whether we allow social intelligence to lead our actions in our families, or on how we decide to express our genders in our families and other social settings.

Because of the significance of our families in developing and increasing our social intelligence, we need to consider patterns in our families' interactions at the same time that we decide where our gender responsibilities lie. For example, we see ourselves more clearly when we examine ways in which our family members interpret their own gender responsibilities, whether or not their gender assumptions are defined and dealt with openly. Our families also show us how gender is presented and discussed with members of younger generations, and whether or not adult family members pay attention to the power and complexities of genders in formulating their own sexual orientations and goals.

Respecting gender responsibilities in our families—by looking at what exists as well as what we would like to accomplish—is a valuable guide to increasing and understanding our social gender and sexual responsibilities. We increase meaning in our lives when we make decisions according to our gender and sexual priorities, for example, or decide to change our gender and sexual identities. We are also more socially intelligent when we use our gender responsibilities to increase the common good and social justice, so that our families, societies, and the world become stronger in the present for the future.

Gender Fulfillment

Social intelligence frequently links our personal, professional, and political accomplishments directly to the fulfillment we experience in our families. Also, our past experiences of fulfillment—perhaps as a child—influence how open and concerned we are to achieve fulfillment today, especially gender fulfillment. For example, when we consider whether or not our family members aim to be fulfilled in their lives, we see more clearly why and how we were oriented toward expecting fulfillment or not.

Social intelligence helps us to understand that our senses of fulfillment are directly related to living meaningfully, and to working toward our preferred goals. For example, when we orient our day-to-day behavior by choosing our most significant values to inform our decisions, as well as work toward our most meaningful goals, we prepare ourselves to be fulfilled. Furthermore, social intelligence guides us to understand our families more fully, so that we discover what it is that we need to be fulfilled.

II. Families and Gender

Reviewing particular aspects of our families' interactions, such as how we were encouraged to learn about the world when we were young, helps us to deal with many complex options to find and express meanings in our everyday lives. How did our parents encourage us—or not—to do well in school? How did relatives express interest—or not—in our earliest achievements? What do we want to accomplish? What do we think we can accomplish? Do our relatives give us strong examples of what to do and what not to do in order to be fulfilled?

This research on our families is invaluable, because it shows us why we think and act in the ways we do, and how we can adjust our thinking and commitments to more closely represent what we want to accomplish for others as well as ourselves. We continue to be rooted in our families, whether we want to be so or not, and we scrutinize our deepest orientations when we choose to educate ourselves about how our families set goals to be fulfilled in past generations.

Even when our family research yields disappointing results, we often become more motivated to change some of the dynamics in our current families, so that we can pursue more meaningful goals. However, these changes should not interrupt how other family members lead their lives. Rather, our relatives ultimately benefit from letting us pursue whatever is most meaningful to us in the long run. For example, aiming for gender fulfillment may include reorienting our personal lives, by changing our assumptions about genders, sexualities, and sexual orientations.

When we make powerful intimate decisions of this kind, our actions necessarily affect our relationships with relatives. Gender and sexuality are strong influences in our social exchanges, so actions involving both gender and sexuality have significant consequences for all family members. For example, social intelligence reminds us that interdependence is a major characteristic of family emotional systems, and that whatever we do affects other family members as well as ourselves.

Social intelligence also shows us that when we aspire to be fulfilled, and seek to express gender fulfillment in how we act, we gradually benefit other family members as well as us. Although our relatives may initially object to our new views of genders, sexualities, and sexual orientations, they are often persuaded by the constructive results of our actions. For example, when we are more fulfilled by the new strategies we use in relation to genders, sexualities, and sexual orientations, we set precedents that others can follow. Success breeds success, and to the extent that we increase our gender fulfillment, our relatives are more likely to increase their gender fulfillment.

One of the most significant ways in which social intelligence sheds light on genders, is to show us how to structure and aim for our own gender fulfillment. When we understand that our actions flow from our value choices, for example, we pay more attention to the kinds of value choices we make, and how they create new baselines for our gender fulfillment and social conditions.

Thus, gender fulfillment is not a haphazard, arbitrary accomplishment, but rather a consequence of deliberate processes that expand and express our social intelligence. When we make more enlightened value choices in the social spheres of families, beliefs, social classes, cultures, and societies, we increase possibilities for gender fulfillment, especially when we start by understanding that our families are instrumental in accomplishing our goals.

III. Beliefs and Gender

Our genders are strongly influenced by our beliefs, just as our beliefs are strongly influenced by our genders. These complex relationships among social influences are clarified through social intelligence, because our deepest beliefs define how we see ourselves, others, and the world. For example, our world views derive from series of values and beliefs that we have tried and tested, often from our earliest childhood. This means that our orientations to gendered beliefs may be impacted critically by multigenerational beliefs, actions, and relationships.

Social intelligence is defined through some of the strongest beliefs we hold, because these flow directly from our experiences of family dependencies, social classes, cultures, and societies. Therefore, when we are socially intelligent about our genders, we need to be aware of our gender beliefs, as well as of how we act according to our gender beliefs and social beliefs.

For example, we must see and understand how our gender beliefs guide us toward futures not yet realized. This means that we benefit from assessing the extent to which our gender beliefs allow us to express our genders meaningfully and sufficiently in our personal relationships, professional accomplishments, and political actions. We do this because our gender beliefs influence us at all times and in all places, whether we want this to be so or not.

Our beliefs about genders create gender identities in ways which have significant social consequences. For example, our gender identities are deep motivators for making decisions and establishing priorities—personally, professionally, and politically. Social intelligence encourages us to monitor our gender beliefs carefully, largely because of the powerful impacts they have on our identities, behavior, and goals. To the extent that social intelligence sheds light on the constructiveness or destructiveness of our gender beliefs, we become freer to decide whether or not to change our gender beliefs and gender identities in strategic ways, and gain control over our preferred objectives and value choices.

How we define our genders and establish meaningful gender identities have major consequences for our sexualities and sexual orientations. Even though our genders are sometimes more directly related to our social intelligence than to our sexualities and sexual orientations, understanding our gender identities often reveals more options for expressing our sexualities and sexual orientations in personal, professional, and political milieus. The self knowledge we use, which derives from our gender beliefs, strengthens our capacities to make decisions about our sexualities and sexual orientations.

An important aspect of allowing social intelligence to guide and express our genders is acknowledging the many choices we have as we live and practice our genders. When we are socially intelligent we take full advantage of this freedom in our choices and actions, by selecting values that guide and express our genders authentically. For example, social intelligence encourages us to increase the meaningfulness of our everyday lives, in order to accomplish constructive goals like increasing the common good and social justice.

Our beliefs and genders have these significant social consequences due to the intensity of the emotions we invest in being men and women, or in having particular sexualities. Important aspects of the physiological base of our gendered behavior are the deep emotions expressed in our identities as men and women, and in our sexualities or sexual orientations. For example, because we already noted the emotional intensity that families bring to bear on genders, sexualities, and sexual orientations, we now see that being socially intelligent helps us to more accurately assess emotional reactivity about genders and sexualities in our communities, social classes, cultures, societies, and globalization.

III. Beliefs and Gender

The fact-based knowledge of social intelligence enables us to size up and use the social realities of our genders and sexualities to our advantage, that otherwise may impinge on us in personal, professional, and political contexts. For example, we begin to see more clearly how historical international trends in genders affect the ranges of our choices in genders and sexualities. This also helps us to understand the broad and deep social roots of our gender beliefs.

Acknowledging these complexities, which is necessary if we are to be socially intelligent in our thinking and actions, gives us more options and control over our everyday choices. For example, as pragmatists we are committed to learning as much as we can about the fact-based social realities of our genders and sexualities, so that we are responsible historical actors who increase the common good and social justice.

Gender Defined

In many respects we define our genders through beliefs that motivate us to act in particular ways. As with other aspects of our identities, we are who we are because of our chosen values and convictions—that is, those deepest beliefs which often remain unquestioned in most social situations. For example, we may continue to nurture and cherish our strongest gender beliefs, without realizing that they are largely absorbed from others rather than developed independently.

The assumptions we make about genders define social realities, as well as our gendered beliefs and actions. For example, we often make conventional assumptions about polarized gender beliefs and gender identities: men are what women are not in infinite variations, just as women are what men are not. Because we unquestioningly believe our assumptions about the complementarity of genders, we develop distinctively distorted world views. Furthermore, even though we both consciously and unconsciously choose our gender beliefs, our gendered beliefs necessarily go before us to create our present and future worlds.

So how does social intelligence change our very real connections to our gendered beliefs and gendered identities? Can social intelligence help us to define our gender beliefs, so that we are freer from their consequences now than in the past? Must we consider genders as polar opposites, or can we define our genders more accurately in idiosyncratic ways? How is social intelligence more than awareness about our gender beliefs? How does social intelligence influence actions generated by our gender beliefs?

First, it is socially intelligent as well as socially significant to question our gender beliefs from many different angles. If we take our gender definitions and gender identities for granted, we automatically maintain the status quo of genders in societies, and at the same time stay stuck in current definitions of the social realities of genders in our everyday situations. Therefore, a first step in becoming more socially intelligent about our genders is to know what our gender beliefs are, and why we have continued to define genders in these ways.

One of the most practical means to understand our gender beliefs is to examine their origins in relation to the major social influences of families, beliefs, social classes, cultures, and societies. For example, we see whose gender beliefs we have absorbed to give us our gender identities, especially in order to adapt to gender definitions and gender values through time. This allows us to begin to assess our gender beliefs, so that we define our genders more broadly, and at the same time work toward goals that are less restricted by gender values that we previously took for granted.

Social intelligence plays an essential role in defining and assessing genders. For example, our new socially intelligent gender definitions and gender identities define our present and futures differently, so that we are freer to contribute to the common good and social justice. Reviewing and revising our genders, according to social intelligence principles, allows us to see new opportunities to develop our preferred gender definitions and goals.

Our effectiveness in strengthening our deliberately chosen gender identities and gender goals is increased by being more socially intelligent. For example, social intelligence strengthens our capacities to be objective, so that we decide more freely what to do, and which commitments to make, without the negative or destructive impacts of conventional gender definitions from our families, beliefs, social classes, cultures, and societies. Social intelligence also clears our thinking about gender and gender definitions, so that we are less likely to become victims in our gendered social situations.

To the extent that we continue to work on being socially intelligent about our genders, we choose to become responsible historical actors who make commitments to free others from their restrictive gendered social realities. For example, we are motivated to open up opportunities for people of different genders and sexualities in education or occupations where discrimination occurs. This action pioneers constructive trends to rebuild our societies, so that genders are no longer expressed automatically in social prejudices that limit some but not others.

We keep these constructive influences in motion by maintaining our awareness of gender beliefs in how we define our genders and ourselves. We cannot afford to go to sleep on this job, because the social consequences are too dire when we continue to take polarized, conventional gender definitions for granted. For example, social intelligence teaches us that we are responsible for the gender worlds we have, and for future gender identities. It is only by making mature decisions about how we define our beliefs about genders now, that we can make long term improvements in gender conditions in our societies.

Gender and Sexuality

One particular belief which influences us all is how gender, which is learned behavior, is linked to sexuality, which has strong physiological components. For example, we often understand genders by believing that they have instinctive sexual roots. Consequently, we may believe that gendered behavior is largely produced by biological urges or instincts, because we think that sexuality is a necessary foundation of genders.

Social intelligence loosens our understanding of some of these linkages between our genders and sexualities, because then we gain more freedom to negotiate our gendered behavior with others. For example, social intelligence helps us to see that we are not biologically determined by our genders, but rather that we have the freedom to choose how to express our genders and sexualities in our everyday activities.

Even though sexualities are linked in some ways to our genders, we can decide not to accept narrow definitions of bipolar sexualities as a basis for understanding the complexities of our genders. For example, when we deliberately consider sexualities in different time periods and contrasting cultures, we see great diversity in how both sexualities and genders are expressed.

Social intelligence increases our objectivity about our social situations and our gendered behavior. Although it may be relatively easy to agree that our actions are not driven by sexual instincts at all times, we also need to acknowledge the omnipresent power of sexualities and genders in our decisions, actions, and commitments. Scrutinizing what we take for granted in our gender definitions of us and other people, for example, allows us to be more innovative in how we interact.

When sexual orientations are used as bases for social classes, majorities and minorities in societies tend to align themselves differently in trying to protect what are considered to be the rights and responsibilities of particular genders and sexualities. However, making socially intelligent commitments to increase the freedom of all, with regard to gender and sexuality, neutralizes some gender and sexuality vested interests. For example, we learn how to respond to major differences in gender and sexuality by expanding our gender definitions to include varieties of sexualities. This is a meaningful goal to strive for, which at the same time broadens and opens up our gender definitions and gender identities.

In the same way that we have already examined our beliefs and gender definitions, our beliefs in gender and sexuality need to be considered in the social contexts of families, general beliefs, social classes, cultures, and societies. Thereby, we acknowledge who in our families, general beliefs, social classes, cultures, and societies has influenced our beliefs in genders and sexualities, as well as whether we are restricted or liberated by our beliefs in genders and sexualities. When we identify problematic restricted beliefs about our genders and sexualities, we recognize that some social attitudes need to be changed, in order to maintain objectivity and socially intelligent freedom for all.

Social intelligence points out the important fact that whatever our beliefs are about our genders and sexualities, we can change them. Even though we have often nurtured and developed our beliefs about genders and sexualities unconsciously rather than deliberately, possibilities to modify or reverse these beliefs about gender and sexuality persist. We are who we are in large part because of our gender beliefs, but we can also change some of our beliefs about the significance of physiological influences on gender and sexuality.

Breaking down dualities in our expectations about genders and sexualities reveals new horizons that make considerable differences in how we live each day. In the long run, we need to make decisions about which gender definitions and which sexualities serve us best in whatever we want to accomplish in our families, communities, societies, and globalization. Although these goals can be reached in varied ways, we often find that we take control of our lives more effectively when we choose how to guide and express our genders and sexualities, so that we can more predictably increase the common good and social justice.

Social intelligence is characterized by broad views of our genders and sexualities. For example, we embrace responsibilities as historical actors more fully when we continue to assess our gender and sexuality roots and goals. These broad views liberate us from being trapped in rigid patterns of gender and sexual behavior in our everyday exchanges with others, so that we become sufficiently free to accomplish our preferred goals for genders and sexualities.

Gender and Sexual Orientation

Although gender and sexuality are social characteristics that are assigned to us all in our families, beliefs, social classes, cultures, and societies, sexual orientation is often more of a hidden attribute or category that we take for granted. For example, sexual orientation is less obvious in our everyday observations than gender or sexuality. Furthermore, because sexual orientation is usually expressed in more intimate forms of behavior than gender and sexuality, we may more easily hide it from others if we want to keep this information private.

Thus, in some respects sexual orientation can be thought of as chosen behavior according to whether or not we let others know what our sexual orientations are. However, because sexual orientation is widely considered to be a primary biological fact of our being, we may believe that most aspects of our sexual orientations and related behavior cannot be changed. For example, we may be who we are due to physiological, biological, or genetic sexual orientations, so that the only real choice we have is whether or not we let others know what our sexual orientations are. Nevertheless, issues of secrecy and taboos, about both minority and majority sexual orientations, are socially significant and worthy of socially intelligent action. This is so because individuals and groups who are not members of mainstream sexual orientations predictably suffer from prejudice and discrimination, as well as risk being harmed by themselves or others.

Gay and lesbian sexual orientations are often kept private in emotional climates where social stigmas are routinely attributed to homosexual people. By contrast, it is relatively easy to act on information about heterosexual orientations, because at present this is the sexual orientation of most people in modern Western societies. Furthermore, the majority of heterosexual people often strives for as much conformity as possible to heterosexual values, which reinforces the social stigmas given to people with homosexual orientations.

Negative social sanctions about homosexual orientations tend to make heterosexuals believe that they are superior to homosexuals. This leads to the establishment or maintenance of social classes that place homosexuals in lower social classes than heterosexuals, and also increases friction among other social classes not directly concerned about the physiology of sexual orientation.

Social intelligence heightens our awareness of the social complexities in genders and sexual orientations. For example, when we are socially intelligent we see contradictions between the facts of sexual orientations and mistaken beliefs, stereotypes, stigmas, sanctions, and prejudices about sexual orientations. Social intelligence also allows us to see more clearly what we can change about our given situations, as well as what we cannot change. Therefore, social intelligence gives us the knowledge and freedom necessary to be strategic in identifying our sexual orientations and our preferred goals.

At best, social intelligence educates and enlightens our beliefs about genders and sexual orientations. For example, we can always learn more about the extent to which our genders and sexual orientations influence us, and how much others' gender or sexual orientation rights and responsibilities need to be respected and protected. However, because we often do not readily acknowledge many inequalities related to genders and sexual orientations, much work needs to be done to expose patterns of prejudice and discrimination that limit our genders and sexual freedom.

Above all, we need to pass on socially intelligent truths about genders and sexual orientations to others, particularly to our children and their children. For example, we cannot change societies without making sure that members of the youngest generations accept sexual diversity more fully than past generations. These social facts are integral parts of social intelligence, which ensure that more productive futures will eventually be created.

We use social intelligence to solve problem issues about genders and sexual orientations, so that many different kinds of individual and social change can take place. Even though choosing to use new values about genders and sexual orientations will not solve all social problems, we can make considerable headway in reorganizing our community and national priorities, when we pay attention to the basic social issues about our beliefs in genders, sexualities, and sexual orientations.

Social intelligence shows us that sexual orientation is not merely a concern for consenting adults. For example, many social issues and social problems result from our beliefs about homosexuality, and different layers of negative emotional reactivity are expressed in community responses to unconventional sexual orientations and practices. However, only when we value sexual diversity in our beliefs about sexual orientations, are we able to construct new societies that strive for social justice, rather than reproduce artificial or destructive patterns of sexual conformity. When we cultivate beliefs that appreciate human differences in whatever we do and accomplish, the world is transformed gradually into more constructive ways of being and acting.

Gender Choices

Gender choices are a privilege that exists for all people, whether we are aware of this or not. Moreover, even our most traditional gender identities can be changed by making decisions and commitments to do things differently, so that improved social conditions are created in the present for the future. Using social intelligence to understand gender beliefs increases our options to express genders each day. Social intelligence also makes us more committed to seek gender opportunities that will create freedoms we do not yet fully understand.

Even though it may appear that we are merely born into our genders and gender identities, we have many gender choices to make if we are to live fully today. For example, our shared existential challenges inspire us to use wide ranges of opportunities and capacities to express ourselves in our complex worlds. These significant social issues remind us that what appear to be our gender experiences are not always what our real situations are, or what our social conditions need us to be and do.

Social intelligence prompts us to cultivate our awareness of the complexities and power of the five major social influences of families, beliefs, social classes, cultures, and societies. When we do this for sufficiently long periods of time, we deepen our understanding that who we are and what we do are largely affected by these complex, powerful, social pressures. Ideally, this awareness inspires us to make more effective concerted efforts to minimize or even neutralize the impacts of these five major social influences on our decisions and commitments to bring our gendered priorities into being.

Our beliefs about genders and gender-related activities are strongly influenced by our family dependencies, social classes, cultures, and societies. Social intelligence suggests that whatever we do results from our gendered understanding of the world. This is so because unless we make deliberate efforts to strengthen our social intelligence, we cannot escape the pervasiveness of the complex and powerful social realities of gender in how we think, how we assess our social situations, and how we act.

Our efforts to increase our social intelligence make us less vulnerable to the insidiousness of gender influences in our lives. Only when we stay aware and discriminating in our gender choices to live as freely as possible, can we be sure that our actions are guided by our strongest gender preferences. For example, socially intelligent gender beliefs increase our ways to be socially intelligent. We free our beliefs from our original gender conditioning, increase our gender choices, and expand others' freedom as well as our own.

When we cultivate beliefs and gender beliefs that strengthen our understanding of families, social classes, cultures, and societies, we increase our resistance and immunity to the power of these major social influences in our everyday lives. Furthermore, when we heighten our awareness of the significance of gender in societies, we clarify our thinking and actions about possibilities for social change beliefs that increase gender freedom and opportunities in societies.

Ideally social intelligence changes not only our awareness of genders in our personal, professional, and political worlds, but also our interests in constructive actions. For example, we use social awareness about genders to bring about changes that increase the common good and social justice. As we increase our social intelligence, we become more responsible historical actors, who are committed to enabling others to benefit from gender beliefs and gender changes that increase gender freedom in the world at large.

A constructive starting point in the creative cycle that brings about gender changes is to focus on our gender beliefs and the historical origins of how we absorbed these beliefs. When we understand the complexities and power of our existing gender beliefs more fully, we begin to deliberately nurture constructive gender beliefs that make us the strongest women and men we can be, and increase gender freedoms in both modern and traditional worlds.

Our gender beliefs are changed in these ways because they did not previously reflect social realities. When the social facts of our gendered situations are more accurately reflected in our gender identities, we see what we need to do to accomplish goals that increase the gender freedom of others as well as ourselves. For example, we work with people who have similar goals, in order to express our changed gender beliefs in effective actions that create significant individual, community, national, and international changes in social conditions.

Gender Responsibilities

Just as we can choose among many varied gender beliefs, we can also choose to be responsible or not with regard to gendered beliefs and actions. For example, at the same time that we increase our social intelligence, we become more aware of what it means to nurture particular gender beliefs that increase or decrease our responsible actions.

We assume gender responsibilities because of the gender beliefs we choose. For example, we choose gender beliefs which help us to act productively with members of our families, so that we concentrate our energies more effectively on meeting their needs as well as our own. When we are responsible in socially intelligent ways, we reduce family dramas—particularly how we react in relation to our most difficult family members—and become more constructive in formulating goals that improve social conditions for all family members, especially by supporting our more dependent, vulnerable family members.

Social intelligence heightens our awareness about our gender beliefs, and the many ways in which gender beliefs influence how responsible we are. Social intelligence encourages us to assess our gender beliefs from the point of view of responsibility, so that we become more inclined to foster gender beliefs that lead us to contribute to the common good or social justice. In other words, we understand the social consequences of our gender beliefs more fully when we are socially intelligent, which makes us more likely to cultivate gender beliefs that have constructive social consequences.

In these respects, social intelligence encourages us to give attention to the broadest contexts of our gender beliefs. Although we need to take care of our own family needs before we try to make specific contributions to the common good and social justice, eventually social intelligence prompts us to meet more general social needs. When we find appropriate ways to do this, we meet our gender responsibilities.

Social intelligence clarifies the distinctions we make between personal and social gender beliefs, which allows us to be more responsible in our actions. For example, we are more responsible when we choose gender beliefs that motivate us to meet general needs in our populations as well as personal gender needs. We move beyond the narrow special interests of our middle class lifestyles, by making gender choices as responsible citizens and socially intelligent historical actors. Moreover, we contribute to the common good as we consider different gender beliefs in our cultures, together with their broad social consequences.

Social intelligence guides our gender awareness, decisions, and commitments in order to become increasingly responsible in our actions. However, our lives are not filled only by seriousness of purpose. Rather, we do whatever we can to be responsible in our choices and actions, especially given the particular social conditions of our populations. Thus, increasing our social intelligence leads us to be more responsible in our gender beliefs and social actions.

We express our responsibilities in choosing and implementing our gender beliefs, by making sure that they motivate us effectively to achieve our preferred goals. We also work to develop gender beliefs that sustain our efforts to reach our goals over long periods of time. Furthermore, because we choose or reinforce values such as equality, inclusiveness, diversity, cooperation, and openness, our gender beliefs ultimately create better futures for our societies.

In the long run, gender beliefs become part of the knowledge of social facts which we absorb as we become more socially intelligent. Our beliefs in social principles—such as holding responsible beliefs in order to create meaning and live fully—gradually become what we know, rather than merely what we believe. However, because we are ever-vulnerable to being distracted from acting according to our most responsible gender beliefs, we must practice reconfirming and strengthening our responsible gender beliefs and choices on a daily basis.

From the point of view of social intelligence, the existential issue of committing ourselves to assuming gender responsibilities does not suggest that we have to be over-responsible in our actions. For example, our genders do not require us to assume responsibilities for others at all times, but rather only when we consider that this is appropriate or needed. We also try not to assume supernatural qualities, like being responsible for all people, but rather choose courses of action selectively that are constructive, because they achieve peaceful co-existence in our gendered worlds.

Gender Fulfillment

Because beliefs are one of the five major strands of social intelligence, cultivating appropriate gender beliefs is a catalyst in bringing about gender fulfillment. For example, when our gender beliefs are in line with our strongest and deepest priorities we function well, know what we are about, and achieve our most important goals. These vital social consequences of our attitudes and actions, are a measure of our success in living according to socially intelligent principles to gain gender fulfillment.

III. Beliefs and Gender

Gender fulfillment through gender and general beliefs, is a critical dimension of our overall fulfillment as human beings. We crave to be fulfilled as gendered individuals, because gender is a deep and emotional part of our human and cultural heritages. Thus, our beliefs about genders, sexualities, sexual orientations, gender choices, and gender responsibilities play crucial roles in our gender identities and gender fulfillment.

It is not possible to achieve ideal goals for gender fulfillment when our beliefs are stuck in unproductive or destructive definitions of genders, sexualities, sexual orientations, gender choices, and gender responsibilities. For example, when any of these social spheres which express our genders is not sufficiently free, we limit our gender fulfillment by continuing to work with false or weak gender beliefs. We need to reflect on gender beliefs in families, social classes, cultures, and societies, in order to understand and act upon our genders, so that our gender beliefs balance and support our experiences of genders and sexualities.

Gender fulfillment through our beliefs calls for the close scrutiny of whatever it is that we want to accomplish most in our lives. This makes us address straight on not only what we need to survive, but also what we want our lives to mean ultimately to ourselves and others. This prompts us to build beliefs that transcend at least some of the mundane everyday needs and gender beliefs which we and our families have now, for example, in order to give sufficient attention to gender goals directly related to the common good and social justice.

Therefore, social intelligence and gender beliefs require us ultimately to serve humankind in ways that evoke our strongest and most constructive values. For example, we try to make value choices which guide us to create social conditions that improve the life chances of most members of our populations. Consequently, we believe that we make significant differences in people's gender fulfillment when we strengthen ideals in our beliefs which express value choices such as equality, inclusiveness, diversity, cooperation, and openness.

We use social intelligence not only to cope with ongoing everyday social pressures, but also to be enlightened about which gender ideals to cherish. For example, can we realistically expect that people want to learn more about their genders, in order to dispel ignorance? Or, is the status quo of traditional beliefs about gender and sexuality reproduced largely because people do not want gendered social realities to be different from those experienced in the past and present?

As we increase our social intelligence, our assessments about what is possible for gender fulfillment become more realistic. For example, we expect more from ourselves and others when we experience advantages from being socially intelligent, and refuse to settle for a status quo of unsatisfying gender and sexual experiences. Social intelligence helps us to accept that gender and sexuality are important aspects of our individual and social fulfillment, and that we must make private and public constructive value choices about equality, inclusiveness, diversity, cooperation, and openness in order to reach our most satisfying goals.

Examining and changing our most cherished beliefs is a valuable stepping stone toward experiencing more holistic gender and general fulfillment. For example, we cannot afford to ignore our strongest gender beliefs, or leave them to stagnate, because these beliefs may block or destroy our attempts to reach our most meaningful goals to increase the common good and social justice.

Even when we attain some degree of gender fulfillment through our gender beliefs, we must continue to increase gender fulfillment through our families, social classes, cultures, and societies. These different perspectives make our social intelligence strong and versatile, which allows us to apply social intelligence principles in any area of our individual and social lives. Only in these circumstances can we become responsible and fulfilled historical actors, who cooperate with like-minded others to achieve the common good and social justice.

IV. Social Classes and Gender

Social classes are another strand of social intelligence which helps us to understand and act in more constructive ways in relation to our genders, sexualities, and sexual orientations. From the point of view of social intelligence, patterns in social classes are one of the five major social influences in societies that impact our lives the most: families, beliefs, social classes, cultures, and societies. Therefore, we need to examine some of the most significant ways in which social classes affect our genders, sexualities, and sexual orientations.

Social classes divide our populations according to social facts such as material assets, occupations, social honor, social connections, race, gender, sexual orientation, age, ethnicity, and religion. We often view ourselves and other people through these social differences, and may plan our daily activities around maintaining our social statuses, or on becoming upwardly socially mobile according to general or gendered social class standards. This suggests that we often choose to focus our energies on improving our social class positions, sometimes especially in relation to social classes based on particular genders, sexualities, and sexual orientations.

In light of these tendencies, social intelligence teaches us to become more objective about those gendered social classes we identify with the most. For example, social intelligence shows us that when we are detached from our most pressing vested interests in upward gendered social class mobility, we can more accurately assess the value or destructiveness of gendered social classes in our everyday lives.

When we use social intelligence to be critical about the coercive influences of gendered social classes with regard to our value choices, we begin to question and challenge the status quo of our gender and sexual social class standards. Our enlightened questioning of the social realities of gendered social classes reveals more choices about the extent to which gender social classes dominate our thinking, decisions, and actions.

Realizing that social intelligence increases our options, through helping us to examine our families and beliefs more objectively, we start to understand more about how social classes define our genders, sexualities, and sexual orientations. For example, by concentrating on the choices we currently make about our genders, sexualities, and sexual orientations, we examine our gender responsibilities more fully. Furthermore, when we try to meet our gender responsibilities according to socially intelligent views of social classes, we see that this may improve our gender fulfillment.

Social intelligence sheds light on the many powerful complexities of social classes with respect to genders, and how social classes affect and even imperil our habitual gender choices. Moreover, when we focus on social intelligence rather than gender or sexual orientation differences, we find similarities among people's basic gender needs which bring the common good into sharper focus. At the same time, our gender and sexual differences help us to appreciate both diversity and inclusiveness, so that we are freer to make responsible gendered decisions about how we live.

Considering gendered social classes broadens our perspectives on our lives, even though contrasts in the experiences of people with different genders, sexualities, or sexual orientations frequently make us feel helpless about changing gendered social classes. All things being equal, we become more strategically situated when we see ourselves in relation to history and broad social changes, especially in recognizing that social classes are directly related to our genders, sexualities, and sexual orientations.

In many respects, one of the greatest strengths of social intelligence is its capacity to transform our understanding of daily life. Social intelligence emphasizes the necessity of using broad social perspectives to understand who we are and what we want to accomplish, so that examining gendered social classes clarifies our thinking about the influences of power and social advantage in our everyday decisions. For example, we see more clearly the cruel contrasts among gendered social classes that support unfair privileges in populations, where some groups have narrowly restricted opportunities and others do not.

Considering the power of social classes based on genders, sexualities, and sexual orientations heightens our awareness about the social injustices maintained by social classes. For example, only when we discover the extent to which lives are harmed by gendered social class differences can we be sufficiently skillful to bring about social changes that increase, rather than limit, opportunities and advantages for all the members of social classes based on genders, sexualities, and sexual orientations.

Understanding gendered social class differences shows us that we need to consider gender needs in assessing our social situations and social conditions. Because we cannot survive in social vacuums, we are compelled to open our eyes and hearts to social facts and social realities about genders, sexualities, and sexual orientations, in order to realize who we are and what we can do through applying social intelligence principles.

Gender Defined

In many respects our social classes help us to define our genders, sexualities, and sexual orientations. We are who we are— as men and women—largely in relation to other social classes of men and women. For example, middle class women are different from upper class women, and at the same time middle class women are different from middle class men, even though having similar financial resources is important in defining how both women and men live day by day.

Gender identity may be defined in terms of how we relate to those who are members of the same or other social classes. Only when we see ourselves and act in relation to varied social classes of men and women, diverse sexual styles, and different sexual orientations can we be objective about our genders. Consequently, all social class and gender aspects of how we see ourselves and the world influence what we do in the present and future.

Social intelligence heightens our awareness of our gender and social class options or possibilities, and guides us to build gender identities that we respect. At best, our gender identities reflect who we really are at deep levels of being and meaning. For example, our ideas about sexualities and sexual orientations emerge from the most profound aspects of our understanding about genders and sexualities. Therefore, we frequently use the tool of social intelligence to clarify our definitions of genders, as well as our identification with particular genders and social classes.

Even though gender social classes may seem to define career choices as well as sexualities, we need to acknowledge the power of sexualities when we heighten our gender awareness. Sexualities are existential means to both reproduce and embrace life's many options. For example, our awareness about sexualities should be balanced by knowing our deepest social concerns about how we make our decisions and commitments. When we are socially intelligent, we do not live merely to squander or dissipate our sexual life forces and energies, but rather to make wise decisions about which gender and sexual social class possibilities we want to pursue through our preferred goals and commitments.

Social intelligence not only heightens our awareness about genders and sexualities, but guides us to accomplish ideals unrelated to upward social class mobility, such as the common good and social justice. In some respects social intelligence is an ideal which suggests that we need to continue to strive to be socially intelligent throughout our lives. For example, we cannot become satisfactorily socially intelligent once and for all. We are responsible for increasing social intelligence and improving social conditions, so that our societies and who we are in the future will be different from what they are today.

Understanding social classes as major social influences yields significant broad perspectives on genders and sexualities. We get to know how other men and women express their genders and sexualities in the world, for example, so that we can be more objective and decisive about which social classes of men and women we belong to, or aspire to belong. Optimally, we grow beyond our social class definitions of genders, because we need to increase the common good and social justice more directly, in order to liberate men and women in their personal relationships and the world at large.

Seeing genders and sexualities, through social classes based on races and ethnicities, gives us other important broad perspectives on genders, as does considering the impacts of social classes based on religions, education, occupations, ablebodiedness, and social connections. All these complex aspects of our genders and sexualities enter into how we define our social classes, as well as influence how we choose our gender identities. Thus, the choices we have in our social situations relate directly to both our genders and our social classes.

Social intelligence continues to shed light on critical gender identity processes, because it connects us to the past, present, and future through our actions and commitments. For example, the more socially intelligent we become, the more effectively we live as historical actors, who establish individual and shared goals to increase the common good and social justice. At best, we use social intelligence to deal with social facts in realizing our goals, so that ultimately we free ourselves from at least some of the restrictiveness of our social classes, genders, and sexualities.

Gender and Sexuality

Gender is often thought of in terms of roles and assumptions that explain social classes as a clear-cut division of lifestyles or work between women and men. For example, because many societies polarize their expectations for men and women, each gender may be defined as being what that other gender is not. Similarly, sexuality is considered to drive the behavior of women and men to some extent, even though in important respects both women and men frequently want to accomplish the same goals, as well as express themselves in similar ways.

Because of widespread trends of sameness in aspirations among both women and men, our dichotomies of male or female gender roles in gendered social classes are largely contrived or meaningless. For example, in order to survive in modern mass societies, we need to understand basic dress and speech codes between and among both women and men, because this gives us the option of building individual differences into how we live our genders and sexualities. Social intelligence helps us to turn possibilities into social realities, and supports us as pioneers who live genders and sexualities differently from the overly simplistic dualistic expectations for gender roles and gendered social classes.

When we appreciate the considerable impacts that social influences have on qualities of our lives, we understand some of the most essential complexities of our genders and sexualities. For example, we see how social classes have different gender and sexuality lifestyles, and we realize that freeing ourselves from some social class goals deepens our experiences of genders and sexualities. We also use social intelligence to be more objective about our genders and sexualities, so that we discover new choices for expressing our genders and sexualities.

In order to nurture the broad perspectives of objectivity that social intelligence brings to understanding genders and sexualities, we examine primary social sources of how we developed our social class genders and sexualities. For example, who assumed leadership responsibilities in educating us about our genders and sexualities in our families? Which family members were our models of femininity or masculinity as we grew to adulthood? Which gender values or sexual lifestyles do we avoid, in order not to get trapped in the intergenerational patterns of genders and sexualities in our families?

Being socially intelligent about our genders and sexualities requires us to research patterns of genders and sexualities in our families, beliefs, social classes, cultures, and societies. Social intelligence focuses on these five major social influences, in order to understand the most significant aspects of our genders and sexualities, because together they create foundations for our experiences in varied social situations, as well as serve as sources of our non-rational gendered behavior. For example, we invest our individual and social emotions most deeply in our families, beliefs, social classes, cultures, and societies, because these are often the most meaningful centers of our everyday lives. How we live each day is important, because experiences enable us to adapt to the rapidly changing circumstances of the modern world and globalization.

Therefore, our genders and sexualities are not purely physiological or biological aspects of our being. Genetics do not dominate the meaning of our life courses, because our bodies react and respond to many complex impacts of the five major social influences of families, beliefs, social classes, cultures, and societies. Furthermore, when we understand these major social influences more fully, we take more control over our lives. Eventually, we become more socially intelligent responsible historical actors, who work productively alone or with others to increase the common good and social justice. Thus, social intelligence supports us to be the best individuals we can be, especially by working with likeminded others to accomplish goals which improve the quality of life for all.

Social intelligence allows us to enjoy our sexualities more freely, rather than experience them as controlling social class influences in our day-to-day lives and destinies. Our socially intelligent choices in genders predispose us to take advantage of the options available to us in modern or traditional societies, so that we are not victims of our own or others' social class sexualities and gender expectations. We use social intelligence to find ways to make our genders and sexualities real by living fully, without impinging on the genders and sexual freedoms of others. Thus genders and sexualities express flexibility and expansiveness, rather than demonstrate servitude to traditional or conventional expectations of gendered social classes.

Gender and Sexual Orientation

Sexual orientation is a significant component of genders, sexualities, and social classes. Although we may choose to keep our sexual orientations private and hidden from others—or even from ourselves—ultimately we need to come to terms with our genders, sexualities, sexual orientations, and social classes, in order to adapt to our social situations and accomplish our preferred goals.

Whatever our sexualities, we often have strong preferences about our sexual orientations. Sexual relationships assume sexual partners, and these patterns of interaction reflect our predispositions to sexual orientations. However, whereas social classes influence sexual behavior in ways that become social class lifestyles, different sexual orientations—when explicit—can be thought of as bases for social classes in their own right, rather than social class lifestyles.

Because minority sexual orientations, such as homosexuality or bisexuality, are not as widespread as the traditional historical sexual orientation of heterosexuality, people with minority sexual orientations tend to be ranked as lower social classes than people with heterosexual orientations. Consequently, genders related to homosexuality are often thought of as being less socially desirable than genders in more widespread heterosexual relationships.

Unfortunately, some family members essentially coerce their children and adolescents to conform to the social class position of the majority sexual orientation of their families or societies. Whereas ideally, sexual orientation is a personal preference that should not—or cannot—be controlled by others, human folly frequently runs rampant in parental efforts to restrict the sexual orientations of their young family members. By contrast, social intelligence gives us both know-how and empathy to support children and adolescents to be who they are, regardless of their particular sexual inclinations. For example, social intelligence helps us to be more objective about our genders and sexual orientations, so that we slowly reduce some of the negative influences of conventional taboos around the wide ranges of sexual orientations in both traditional and modern societies.

Social intelligence requires us to maintain broad, objective perspectives whenever possible, so that we do not miss seeing the whole picture of our lives and social classes. We cannot aim to increase social justice among all people, for example, if we do not support sexual diversity. We must recognize that being different is one of the main social facts of our individual and social lives: we are who we are, and we must accept both who we are and who others are.

Social intelligence gives us sufficient confidence to stand alone, or with others, in our views about genders, sexualities, sexual orientations, and social classes. When we understand that increasing human choices leads to social progress, we embrace gender and sexual diversity more willingly. For example, a vital common good and social justice are achieved when diversity is sought for rather than avoided. When we experience wide varieties of humankind, our sexual orientations express diversity beyond the conventional confines of particular social classes.

In these respects, sexual orientation is part of an ever-increasing diversity, rather than a necessary base for continued social class hierarchies. Social intelligence shows us that we should not stand united to support only vested interests in particular social classes, but rather extend ourselves as historical actors who try to impact all societies. However, we need to recognize relationships among social classes built on sexual orientation, in order to better cooperate with others, as well as work together more effectively to improve gender and sexual orientation statuses in our social relations and globalization.

Just as gender identities and sexualities are best known and expressed through the major social influences of families, beliefs, social classes, cultures, and societies, our sexual orientations need to be addressed in each of these social spheres. Although we cannot claim that our sexual orientations derive solely from these five social sources, we find that how we express our sexual orientations affects and is affected by all these major social influences.

With regard to sexual orientations, our options include how to present ourselves in the world. For example, social intelligence encourages us to voice our concerns about sexual orientation social classes, in order to free ourselves from their more destructive social consequences. Thus, going public with our sexual preferences may help to banish some traditional cultural taboos about minority sexual orientations in the long run, so that we become more effective historical actors who cooperate with others to increase social justice, regardless of—or perhaps because of—their sexual orientations.

Gender Choices

Social intelligence encourages us to make gender choices depending on our knowledge of genders from the five major social influences of families, beliefs, social classes, cultures and societies. When we see complex aspects of genders from the points of view of these five major social influences, we are more objective about our gender identities and gender opportunities, as well as freer to make decisions about genders, sexualities, and sexual orientations.

Examining the major social influence of social classes on genders, sexualities, and sexual orientations shows us the extent to which we restrict our gender choices according to social class expectations and social class aspirations. For example, modern industrial societies base their economies on beliefs such as the benefits of upward social mobility, so that many of our actions focus on achieving sufficient means to move up social class hierarchies. These social class pressures also influence how we see and express our genders, sexualities, and sexual orientations.

Social intelligence draws our attention to the importance of considering connections among social classes, genders, sexualities, and sexual orientations, if we are interested in understanding the true ranges of our gender possibilities. To the extent that an existential goal for most people is to live fully, we are more likely to accomplish this depth and breadth of being when we maintain our awareness of how our actions are affected by others and vice versa.

Instead of thinking that we merely have choices of being males or females who conform to particular standards of behavior, we enrich our experiences by exploring our options in life as holistically as possible. For example, examining ranges of options in families, beliefs, social classes, cultures, and societies opens our eyes to possibilities which we may not have seen before, or which we may have taken for granted.

Social intelligence requires that we question all aspects of our social being, so that we deepen our understanding of how much we follow others' standards of behavior, rather than our own inclinations or deepest beliefs. This is not to encourage rebellion against existing social classes, but rather to cultivate sufficient objectivity to see ourselves and others more clearly for who and what we are beyond social classes.

One key to understanding the difficulties we have in being free, or even in seizing our freedom once we see it, is to acknowledge the emotional dependencies and intensities that charge the five major social influences of families, beliefs, social classes, cultures, and societies. Social intelligence is a way to be more rational about the emotional dependencies in our everyday lives, so that we make meaningful and effective choices about which strategies we use to accomplish our goals. Thus, our choices result from our capacities to be socially intelligent, as well as our interests in being free.

Upper class lifestyles and behavior often express traditional values and beliefs that have been passed down from generation to generation. Although people with independent means have long supported outrageous gender or sexual deviance from traditional standards, usually members of upper social classes have not questioned or transformed conventional definitions of genders, sexualities, and sexual orientations as much as members of lower social classes.

One of the socially intelligent questions to ask about genders, sexualities, and sexual orientations in social classes is how social classes influence or restrict our genders. For example, do we continue men's and women's gender traditions because of social class dictates? How are our occupations and career goals affected by women's and men's gender traditions? Do particular modes of behavior—such as being active or passive—reflect gender traditions? Do we follow gender traditions that restrict our opportunities to live fully in parenting, caring for our parents, or working out of the home?

Social intelligence is a significant means or strategy which shows us the restrictiveness of the five major social influences of families, beliefs, social classes, cultures, and societies. When we bring these forces into balance in our lives, we move more freely within and among these social spheres, so that we accomplish goals which help to free those who are trapped by social class influences. Social classes of genders, sexualities, and sexual orientations inevitably tie us to relatively closed patterns of thinking and social interaction in the long run, unless social intelligence principles guide our behavior.

Ideally, we use social intelligence to increase constructive social goals and productive ways to relate to each other. For example, social intelligence helps us to be responsible historical actors who aim to increase the common good and social justice, because they create equality, inclusiveness, diversity, cooperation, and openness in our societies. Social intelligence also neutralizes various social class influences, so that we focus more effectively on broad social issues—such as unjust inequalities—that need to be addressed in order to benefit all.

Gender Responsibilities

Making choices to be responsible about our genders evokes ranges of specific options in relation to the major social influences of families, beliefs, social classes, cultures, and societies. Furthermore, because being socially intelligent increases our capacities to be responsible, we find that being aware of the power and complexities of these major social influences encourages us to participate in social issues more than before. For example, when we know that what we have learned can be unlearned, possibilities for doing things differently increase. Social intelligence is based on the principle that we are social beings, and that particular impacts of the power and complexities of major social influences can be unlearned.

IV. Social Classes and Gender

Social intelligence sheds light on dark parts of our everyday worlds. We see that social problems, such as social class injustices, are partly related to how we choose to think, believe, and act. For example, our commitments keep some gender inequalities, sexuality contrasts, and sexual orientation tensions in motion or in place. We are responsible for the way things are, how we organize ourselves in social classes, and how things could be in the future.

We assume more gender responsibilities when we understand more fully that we can make different value choices that increase gender freedom for us and others. For example, we use social intelligence to find ways to deal with existing social classes of gender and sexual inequalities, so that all our actions can be more responsible. Therefore, our gender responsibilities often result from the extent to which we recognize the consequences of our gendered actions.

Separating genders from sexualities and sexual orientations helps us to be more in charge of those gender beliefs and gendered social classes that influence our genders, sexualities, and sexual orientations. However, it is easier for us to change our genders than our sexualities and sexual orientations, largely because physiological and biological urges are more directly expressed through our sexualities and sexual orientations. When we focus exclusively on genetic sex drives, we discover that we have limited control over physiological, biological, and social outcomes. By contrast, gender responsibilities based on social intelligence help us to see how differently we may express ourselves physiologically and biologically in particular social situations.

Assuming gender responsibilities neutralizes some of the power and complexities of social class influences on our genders, sexualities, and sexual orientations. Social intelligence guides us to stay sufficiently outside our social class influences, so that we do not automatically follow social class dictates in expressing our genders. For example, we put economic, educational, occupational, racial, ethnic, health, and gender differences to one side as much as possible, when we review our options for gender behavior and decision-making. We also make commitments to better humankind, rather than to increase artificial social class distinctions among boys, girls, men, women, homosexuals, bisexuals, transsexuals, and heterosexuals.

Social intelligence teaches us that being responsible benefits all. For example, when we work with responsible others, we accomplish difficult tasks effectively by cooperating rather than competing. Nevertheless, we need considerable social intelligence in order to be truly responsible, because being responsible for our genders is more difficult than going with the flow of specific social situations.

To the extent that we decide to while away our time and energy, rather than aim to achieve responsible goals, we use up vital life energies without producing social changes that would benefit ourselves and others. Being thoughtless and carefree may be valuable for pure rest and relaxation, but they are not reliable guides for achieving healthy lifestyles or preferred goals. We miss many rewarding experiences when we choose not to educate ourselves about individual and social possibilities, or refuse to be responsible for our genders, social worlds, globalization, and planet earth.

Living our gender responsibilities increases our control over the outcomes of our gender decisions, and enlightens our goals. We grow through our social intelligence, so that we are free to assume demanding gendered tasks, as well as to meet more personal obligations. We also count on others to be responsible as much as possible, in order to coexist peacefully and work together effectively, so that we accomplish what we cannot do alone. Assuming gender responsibilities means that we neutralize some of the more destructive impacts of traditional or conventional gender dualities and gendered social classes. Ultimately, we become stronger women and men who make wise gender choices in expressing socially intelligent gender responsibilities.

Gender Fulfillment

Even though we are often raised to believe that upward social class mobility will bring gender fulfillment, this is usually false.

IV. Social Classes and Gender

Upper social classes are riddled with traditional values about gender, which limit both women and men in their aspirations and accomplishments. For example, traditional gender values assume cultural complementarity between men and women, as well as overly simplistic dichotomies of gender contrasts.

However, if we deliberately decide to conform to traditional gender values, there may be some benefits. Traditional gender identities allow us to adjust and fit into diverse social situations, and we may be bestowed with social honor as long as we conform to the rules for being a "good" woman or a "good" man. In emergencies, or in times of ambiguity, making traditional value choices may well be our wisest course of action. For example, it is realistic to strategize our behavior, so that we can act quickly and without much forethought when necessary.

In the long run, however, social intelligence guides us to be more authentic about who we are as women or men. For instance, when we are self conscious in identifying our genders, sexualities, and sexual orientations, we ground ourselves more securely in social facts of the past, present, and future, than if we follow historical or traditional precedents blindly. Furthermore, when we make socially intelligent gender choices and assume socially intelligent gender responsibilities, we are predictably more fulfilled through our genders.

In these respects, social intelligence teaches us to be cautious and discriminating in selecting both traditional and conventional gender values to guide us. However, we also need to continue to question different aspects of genders, sexualities, and sexual orientations, in order to be sure that our commitments really follow social intelligence ideals to increase the common good and social justice. Questioning our gender value choices helps us to check our progress in accomplishing our goals, which ultimately increases our gender fulfillment.

The processes involved in becoming strong, socially intelligent men and women help us to be wise about allowing selected social class values to influence what we think and do. We also learn how to pay attention to gender influences in our families, beliefs, cultures, and societies, as well as in our social classes, because all five of these major social influences frequently impinge on our freedom as women and men.

Social class influences on genders, sexualities, and sexual orientations are usefully considered from the points of view of understanding patterns of social behavior in ourselves, our communities, our societies, and the world. For example, when social class concerns dominate our decision-making, we need to remind ourselves of the importance of being objective about our social situations, given our strong vested interests. Social intelligence suggests that our greatest gender freedom and gender fulfillment derive from being objective, rather than from reacting to narrow, parochial views of social realities.

In important respects, social intelligence encourages us to go beyond our social classes in developing our genders, sexualities, and sexual orientations. We become more neutral about the social classes we were born into, for example, so that we do not continue to formulate or pursue the same social class goals for decades. Rather, we select new more universal goals that are uniquely meaningful to us, in order to strengthen our everyday purposes. We also modify our social mobility interests, so that we reduce rather than increase social class inequalities.

Although our original social classes are arbitrary beginnings, they are significant vantage points from which to assess our progress in contributing to the socially intelligent goals of the common good and social justice. Aiming to accomplish these ideals enhances our fulfillment, and allows us to help others to be fulfilled. Thus, our deeply challenging, responsible gender choices ultimately carve out increased gender fulfillment and life satisfaction.

Our greater understanding of social class impacts on genders, sexualities, and sexual orientations suggests connections between our personal experiences, cultures, and societies. For example, we realize that our own situations are linked to national and international cultures, as well as to globalization. International social class differences and contrasts show us how families and

IV. Social Classes and Gender

beliefs may support or re-design social classes, so that gender choices remain central in our gender fulfillment, wherever we are and whatever we are doing. Furthermore, social intelligence guides us to constantly expand our horizons, so that we contribute to the world at large at the same time that we meet our individual and family needs.

V. Cultures and Gender

Cultures are the fourth of the five major social influences that strongly affect our genders, sexualities, and sexual orientations. For example, cultures are made up of values, standards, ideals, ideas, knowledge, expectations, religions, laws, education, sciences, and symbols. We find meaning in our lives because of our cultures, and our cultures are found everywhere in our societies and personal interactions with others. For pragmatic reasons we need to absorb parts of our cultures, in order to know how to conduct ourselves in different situations in societies, and we usually choose our goals according to our dominant cultural values.

Our families have cultures, our beliefs are part of our cultures, and our social classes are supported by social class cultures. Therefore, we find many overlapping cultures when we examine the five major social influences in societies. Because families, beliefs, social classes, cultures, and societies are connected to widespread emotional needs of populations and societies, cultures run deep in our being. For example, we are not considered to be fully human unless we learn successfully from our cultures.

As we grow to adulthood, we often become increasingly aware that our genders, sexualities, and sexual orientations have different cultures. This does not mean that our genders, sexualities, and sexual orientations are caused by our cultures, but rather that our cultures are powerful aspects of who we are, the genders we choose, our sexualities, and our sexual orientations. Furthermore, social intelligence suggests that when we understand these social facts, we gain more control over who we are, what we do, and how we create constructive futures.

Cultures motivate us both to conform to others' expectations and to pursue our own ideals. Cultures are the substance of our education and learning, and social intelligence can be thought of as a cultural ideal to which we may aspire. For example, we try to become more socially intelligent because we find meaning through pursuing purposeful goals.

As well as being a major social influence in our everyday lives, cultures reveal possibilities for changes. When we increase our social intelligence, for example, we heighten our awareness of the value choices we make. Moreover, if we conclude that we have needlessly restricted ourselves through our value choices, we begin to realize that we need to make different value choices now. Thus, values such as equality, inclusiveness, diversity, cooperation, and openness may transform our views of who we are, as well as how our genders, sexualities, and sexual orientations are expressed or changed.

Cultural values inspire us, and are reliable means to refresh our purposes. If we get stuck in our everyday patterns of behavior, for example, we can turn to cultures to inform and help us see our social conditions more objectively. We bring improved social conditions into being when we clarify our ideas about alternative values, which may motivate us to pioneer in critical, sensitive areas of our genders, sexualities, and sexual orientations.

New views of our cultures are found in newspapers, books, and diverse media such as fine arts. Social intelligence helps us to discern the functions of our culture, in part because broad social intelligence perspectives make us more aware of how cultures help to subjugate us in social classes, including social classes based on genders, sexualities, and sexual orientations. For example, when we realize the many ways in which we conform to different social classes, we may begin to free ourselves by choosing new options rather than repeating our daily rituals.

The complex and powerful inner cultural conditioning of our genders encourages us to define genders in particular ways. For example, we may have accepted certain givens about how men and women behave, or should behave, as being "natural."

V. Cultures and Gender

Similarly, we often associate specific forms of sexualities with particular genders and sexual orientations. Social intelligence helps us to modify our overly simplistic ways of thinking about genders and sexualities, through a scrutiny of the many cultural choices available to us. Consequently, we may decide to call a halt to the multigenerational cultural conditioning in our families, because we better understand the significance of our present cultural choices.

Seeing cultures as historical choices also opens up new possibilities. For example, we realize who we are today more fully when we compare our lives with those of our ancestors or grandparents. Furthermore, appreciating the impact of time on cultural expectations makes us more objective, so that we assess what we really want to do with our lives more accurately, especially in relation to our genders, sexualities, and sexual orientations. Thus, historical facts do not determine who are in the present, but rather show us what not to do in the present and future.

Gender Defined

Social intelligence helps us to understand the complexity of both our cultures and our genders. When we are socially intelligent we see linkages between our cultures and our genders, and work toward becoming freer in our choices of cultures and genders. We realize that we are who we are because we have learned our genders, and we make wiser gender choices when we discern which gender values and gender symbols are most meaningful to us in our cultures. For example, we may choose to define our genders according to particular clusters of traditional or modern cultural values.

Social intelligence requires us to take our genders seriously, because gender is an important prism through which other people see and hear us. Social intelligence also makes us aware of the many choices we have in expressing our genders, especially through our societies' cultures. We define ourselves, as well as our gender choices, within our cultures because cultural meanings motivate us to act each day, whether we realize this or not.

When we know who we are and what we really care about, we are more discriminating about our gender choices and gender identities. We decide to be particular kinds of men and women, for example, through choosing gender values that we cherish. We may opt to be religious or secular, and learned or ignorant, as well as express other cultural values. The power that flows from being socially intelligent is that we know more about what we do, what we stand for, and where we are going amidst the overwhelming plethora of cultural and gender choices in our societies.

Because we learn our gender values through our cultures on a continuing basis, it is also possible to unlearn gender values through cultures when our original gender values are no longer truly meaningful. The many new ranges of cultural values we can access—for example, throughout history and in contrasting cultures—become wider outer limits of our social intelligence. As long as we are aware of diverse cultural values and cultural styles, we are free to define and identify with fresh gender values differently.

We have the capacity to change our gender identities many times in our lifetimes, or even within an hour. We renew ourselves by engaging in serious assessments of the gender identities that we want to be and do. Thus we are actions as well as actors, and the flow of our actions frequently derives directly from the integrity of our gendered value choices in our cultures. Although our decisions may drive us from task to task, our choices of ideals and goals reflect cultural values and gendered identities.

Our genders strengthen our senses of belonging to societies, especially when we choose mainstream cultural values. We settle into our chosen gender definitions through habitual behaviors, and when we become mature and responsible adults, our gender choices are more discriminating, reflecting the deepest parts of who we are. Thus, in order to live fully, we make it our business to stay as free as possible in our cultural gender choices and gender expressions.

Social intelligence is both a safety net and an inspiration in these bold personal and public ventures. For example, when we choose not to act automatically, or not to take our lives for granted, we are rewarded by forging deeper meanings in our everyday lives. Thus, social intelligence anchors us purposefully in our societies, and frees us to make more selective commitments to build better worlds. These commitments provoke new value choices, because our gender cultures are more robust and vibrant. Furthermore, experiencing this new quality of life readies us to dedicate ourselves more fully to increasing the common good and achieving social justice.

The tasks involved in defining our genders are never complete. However, social intelligence shows us that it is often sufficient merely to choose to go in meaningful directions, because we need to continue to define our genders throughout our lives. Our main existential challenge is to rise above overly narrow definitions of genders, which usually support the vested interests of one gender definition over another. Rather, our socially intelligent goal is to find some meaningful common denominators among the gender choices of all people. It is only by aiming to improve the quality of life for all, for example, that we adequately meet challenges to further the common good and social justice.

Gender and Sexuality

Our cultures tend to constantly dictate new modern standards of sexuality from generation to generation. For example, even though sexual behavior has been acknowledged and discussed in the past, today's cultures have considerably more explicit references to gender and visual symbols of sexuality than most pre-modern societies. In fact, sexualities are often portrayed in current societies as essential aspects of our being and doing. For example, children easily get caught up in dangerous contemporary whirlpools of sexual possibilities, with the result that members of our youngest generations tend to be more interested in wide ranges of sexual options than children in prior generations.

Because of the omnipresence of our cultures, and the pervasiveness of cultural pressures to express sexualities as an important part of our daily lives, transient sexualities may have stronger allures for some people than traditional, institutional courtship and marriage. Whereas there are more gender and sexuality choices today, about whether or not to remain single or celibate, maintaining virginity for both men and women may be more challenging than in prior generations, due to persistent cultural emphases on spontaneous sexualities.

Contemporary cultural perspectives on sexualities also suggest that we need to express sexualities in order to be active in the game of life. For example, we are pressured by our cultures to dress in sexually suggestive ways at all times, in order to be "cool" or trendy sexual beings. Also, our cultures dictate beliefs that we may not be considered healthy unless we have active sexual lives. Thus, we are expected to be sexual whether we are married or not, and whether we have a steady sexual partner or not.

Although we used to assess our genders in relation to traditional cultural expectations of the past, today's cultures pressure us to associate every aspect of our genders with current sexual behaviors, or we run the risk of being considered deviant, ill, or misfits. In these respects, genders and sexualities are embodied in our cultural values and cultural symbols as crucial aspects of the good life, with the result that traditions such as families and celibacy are weakened.

Cultural pressures to be sexual beings are exacerbated and exploited by the material cultures of capitalism in modern societies. Modern consumerism has a cultural hold and power largely because it deliberately reinforces values that are being articulated by our cultures. Thus capitalist material cultures aggravate and increase existing modern cultural trends about sexualities, rather than create completely new or improved cultural worlds. For example, high-powered advertising focuses on young adults who yearn for the good life, and at the same time enables corporations to reap huge profits. Consequently, we need to question and change what we consider the good life to be, if we are to gain more control over current patterns in the cultural dominance of contemporary genders and sexualities.

Social intelligence gives us greater freedom to assess the importance of sexualities in our genders, because we gain objectivity and choose new options when we become more socially intelligent. For example, historical views of sexualities loosen the power that current cultural standards and symbols have over us, because we use broader perspectives on sexualities when we refer to historical facts and experiences. This increased knowledge of social facts strengthens our social intelligence, so that we are no longer as pressured to conform to current sexual standards in modern cultures.

Social intelligence does not deny sexualities, or limit our capacities to be sexual, but rather aligns our particular needs for sexualities today with broad historical views of cultures. Also, becoming historical actors, through applying social intelligence principles to our everyday lives, enhances our senses of self, as well as our capacities to accomplish more of what we believe. For example, we stand up for our sexual preferences more readily, when we are bolstered by knowledge about what was honored in the past as well as the present.

Our discomfort in feeling trapped in present cultural standards of sexualities may motivate us to work with others to change cultural pressures to be sexual at all times. For example, we may try to reduce the impacts of sexual symbols and sexual content in our cultures, when we are more aware of sexual social realities in the present and what they could be in the future. When we maintain this socially intelligent posture, in reviewing our present and future options, we are fortified by cultural values such as freedom and reason, so that we create more viable current and future sexual cultures.

Gender and Sexual Orientation

Cultures continue to be our most significant sources of values and ideals for inspiring and protecting sexual orientations, as well as for genders and sexualities. Although historically social facts show us that some societies accepted homosexuality positively, heterosexuality continues to be consistently more privileged and more practiced over time. For example, even though some contemporary modern societies embrace homosexuality more fully than in previous historic times, homosexuality often continues to be viewed as deviant or "unnatural" by members of social classes in the mainstream of societies.

We make some progress in changing these conventional cultural views of social honor and homosexuality when we make new value choices which enhance social opportunities for lesbian and gay individuals, as well as homosexual communities. For example, social intelligence helps us to understand subtle differences among sexual orientations, as well as the most dominant shared values of homosexual and heterosexual people, which may have previously seemed to be incompatible. However, because cultures continue to present us with new value options, we maintain our socially intelligent responsibility when we consistently select values that strengthen the common good.

We benefit from choosing to honor clusters of values that promote freedom for all—such as equality, inclusiveness, diversity, cooperation, and openness—because both heterosexual and homosexual communities benefit from strengthening these values. Social justice values like this ensure that equal rights are respected, and that we can build future societies safely on solid, reliable moral foundations that respond to universal needs rather than special interests.

Social intelligence guides us in directions which require more aware ethical value choices. For example, social intelligence helps us to increase the common good, so that both homosexual and heterosexual orientations and practices are respected, at the same time that new and stronger moral foundations of societies are built. Optimally, social intelligence increases peaceful coexistence among people with different sexual orientations, so that hate crimes decrease. In fact, only when we value diverse sexual orientations in our societies can we adequately meet the needs of all members of our populations.

Cultures are also resources for individuals and groups who want to nullify some of the artificial dichotomies in genders and sexual orientations. For example, conventional cultural values of femininity and masculinity distort our understanding and actions with regard to both genders and sexual orientations. However, because homosexual people legitimately want as many privileges as heterosexual people in today's societies, we need to clarify our ideas and policies about what it takes to create such social conditions. How do feminine and masculine values influence sexual orientations? What pragmatic considerations must we respect in order to treat people with different sexual orientations equally in our societies?

Existing legislation and policies heighten our awareness about what should be done to bring about more equality between homosexuals and heterosexuals, as well as more gender freedom. However, unless we give sufficient attention to all aspects of sexual orientation inequalities, we may not rectify even the most egregious injustices, or those injustices that are relatively hidden from public view. Significant nuances in minority sexual orientations are difficult to detect, especially by people with mainstream sexual orientations. Nevertheless, we must make socially intelligent efforts to understand these important contrasts in sexual orientations, so that we can honor the cultural value of equality in sexual orientations and genders throughout societies.

One social intelligence principle related to these concerns is that more equal relationships are needed in order to have more sexual fulfillment and opportunities for social contributions. We can only improve future social conditions when we accomplish equality for both survival and fulfillment. Working together to meet universal goals for people of all sexual orientations, allows us to release some of the crippling pressures from inequalities in current social and sexual situations.

Thus, we work more definitively toward better futures for all, when we make the social conditions of different sexual orientations more equal. For example, we show improved qualities in social conditions when people with different sexual orientations are treated well. We cannot hope for better tomorrows for our children, in the important areas of genders and sexualities, if we are reluctant to deal with disturbing contrasts and conflicts in diverse sexual orientations.

Gender Choices

Social intelligence shows us that we can make many gender choices in relation to our cultures, as well as in relation to the other major social influences of families, beliefs, social classes, and societies. Moreover, we continue to have these choices, in spite of the extent to which we may have learned restrictive aspects of social facts in our gendered situations, and from our personal experiences of the complex and powerful influences of families, beliefs, social classes, cultures, and societies.

However, even though we may have routinely accepted these limitations, we can unlearn them, or develop more constructive gender postures in relation to the five major social influences. Given the fact that our current gender identities may be largely defined by our relatively unenlightened choices through the years, social intelligence heightens our awareness about our present options. Social intelligence also suggests new directions that make real differences in our gendered lives, such as aiming to increase the common good or social justice.

Therefore, social intelligence emphasizes the universality of the human condition, and the universality of our choices about genders. In most cases, this increases the options we thought we had as children and adolescents, and adds possibilities for adults who are thoughtful about self and identity. For example, our cultures govern what our value choices are, and clusters of related values usually guide our action in everyday lives. These are the reasons that lead us to scrutinize our cultures, so that we use our most constructive values to make our daily choices and interactions more effective.

Unless we consider ways in which women and men are similar as well as different, we may deny ourselves full ranges of choices as human beings. Thus, examining cultural differences between women and men reveals both superficial and significant differences. For example, women's and men's dress codes do not have as strong impacts on life outcomes as job or career choices. Furthermore, in order to recognize the breadth of our gender choices, we should take into account the immense variety of men and women in contrasting cultures and circumstances.

Social intelligence requires us to stay informed about gender choices, so that we select more educated options about what we really want to accomplish in our lives. For example, we could choose to be committed to increasing gender equity in contemporary societies, or we could pursue atypical goals for men and women because we believe in pioneering cultural innovations. In any event, reviewing our cultural options is refreshing, and needs to be done regularly, if we are to stay true to far-reaching goals like increasing social intelligence in our personal or professional lives, communities, and societies.

Because our cultures are made up of values, ideals, ideas, expectations, religions, knowledge, laws, and beliefs, we see how socially intelligent choices about our genders enhance the meaningfulness of our gender identities and gendered selves. For example, when we deliberately select the values we want to cultivate and strengthen, our everyday lives change. Because our sexualities and sexual orientations are deep aspects of who we are, it is imperative to sort out to what extent our cultural gender choices are priorities in our decision-making and commitments. Knowing which aspects of our cultures we want to nurture, guides our responsible actions toward fulfillment.

Sometimes personal or political crises make us pay closer attention to our gender choices. When we cannot accomplish what we want, we can still choose to see our failures to reach our goals as opportunities to go in new directions. For example, we may choose to be motivated by more conventional cultural choices, so that our efforts become more efficient. Ultimately, however, our cultural resources are needed to replenish our moral fortitude. We renew our faith in values that transcend self, for example, so that we move more effectively in our preferred directions. Thus, more discriminating value choices bring about improved consequences for all.

When we want to be socially intelligent, we try to be more objective about our social situations and options in different social circumstances, so that we broaden our horizons of possibilities. To the extent that we persist in following goals that inspire us and others, we increase social justice today for tomorrow. When we envision our genders in light of values such as equality, inclusiveness, diversity, cooperation, and openness, we build better societies in the present and the future.

Gender Responsibilities

Because our cultures help us to define our values, and are made up of values, we can base our gender responsibilities on whatever inspires us to act wisely in relation to our cultural resources. How have people of different genders, sexualities, and sexual orientations entered into gendered commitments over the years? What is it about gender that predisposes us to conform to cultural standards in our expectations about appropriate behavior or goals? If we want to be socially intelligent and free where others are concerned, can we live a responsibility-free life? Or, do we have to decide which responsibilities we need to assume, because of our particular genders and sexual orientations?

Social intelligence broadens our perspectives and increases our objectivity about gender and sexual responsibility issues. When we recognize the many value choices we have in creating and expressing our gender identities, for example, we tend to be more responsible in making these choices and incorporating them into our everyday lives. Furthermore, social intelligence helps us to be more aware of the consequences of our actions, and their social impacts on others. This deeper understanding makes responsible actions more likely.

Increasing the deliberateness of our gender choices often moves us in directions of being more responsible in our actions, especially when we try to meet socially intelligent goals, such as increasing the common good or social justice. These socially intelligent ideals guide our good intentions, so that we are more effective and more responsible about knowing the outcomes of our plans. Awareness of self, amidst the five major social influences of families, beliefs, social classes, cultures, and societies, helps us to see significant social facts, so that we meet others' needs as well as our own, especially in the spheres of genders and sexualities.

Gender is a deep-seated emotional aspect of who we are, which should not be denied. Therefore, it is not responsible to put concerns about genders and the consequences of our gendered actions to one side. We must continuously ask whether what we do affects our gender identities, or the gendered actions of others. For example, can we protect the gender and sexuality rights of other people as well as our own? Are we sensitive to others' special needs around contested social issues like sexual orientation?

Cultures enlarge the range of traditional and modern options that we have with regard to our gender responsibilities, especially when we compare and contrast our opportunities with those of others. Cultures also reinforce our most cherished gender values, so that we can continue to honor our deep commitments to act forthrightly about genders. Furthermore, only when we understand the cultural complexities of our gender responsibilities do we become fully responsible as human beings.

Our gender responsibilities relate directly to the five major social influences of families, beliefs, social classes, cultures, and societies when we are socially intelligent. Rather than succumb to the power and complexities of these influences, social intelligence shows us how to participate selectively in their pressures. For example, we assume responsibilities in our families as gendered individuals or groups; we scrutinize our beliefs for biases that restrict the gender well-being of others, so that we can have more constructive social impacts; and we minimize social class differences among different genders and sexualities. We also make more knowledgeable cultural choices about our gender responsibilities—including deciding to act responsibly rather than irresponsibly—so that we become responsible historical actors.

When we consider gender responsibilities in socially intelligent ways, we realize that we need to use our cultural choices as wisely as possible at all times. As this is a worthy but impossible goal to aim for, we must be content with making relatively slow progress toward being responsible in our gendered actions. Our chief goal is to use our cultures sufficiently to nurture constructive gender ideals and intentions, so that eventually our actions fall into line with regard to our own gender expectations.

Our intention is not to be partly responsible for some of the time, but rather to be fully responsible all the time. However, we need to allow ourselves some flexibility in these intentions when necessary, in order to ensure that we continue to make our best efforts to assume gender responsibilities through our cultures in the long run. We can depend on social intelligence to be a reliable guide on this meaningful venture, and we do not lose sight of our social justice objectives, because our authentic gender responsibilities drive us forward.

Gender Fulfillment

In important respects, gender fulfillment flows more or less predictably from at least trying to meet our varied gender responsibilities. When we realize that expressing our genders means that we should assume particular responsibilities for others as well as for ourselves, we try to follow this up through our actions, so that we derive fulfillment from accomplishing and aiming to accomplish our goals. For example, when we cooperate with others to formulate and implement policies that improve education for women, men, and children in poor countries, we increase our gender fulfillment because we are increasing social justice as well as the common good. However, by contrast, gender fulfillment does not usually occur if we act randomly, or without particular intentions and goals.

Definitions of our gender responsibilities and gender fulfillment are largely informed by our cultures. Cultures provide us with a rich array of value choices, and we are socially intelligent when we keep our lives on track by selecting values that mean the most to us. At the same time, we benefit from letting social intelligence show us significant social facts about our social situations, so that we aim to create better conditions for the present and future by using social justice values such as equality, inclusiveness, diversity, cooperation, and openness.

Therefore, gender fulfillment is achieved in large part because we stay in control of what we want to accomplish in our lives. For example, when we are careful about selecting and using meaningful values in our cultures, our lives take on purposes and directions that may gradually become missions for a lifetime. Then we not only define our genders and sexualities in ways that we truly choose, but we also make series of commitments to accomplish gendered goals through becoming responsible historical actors.

Gender fulfillment flows from coming to terms with the five major social influences of families, beliefs, social classes, cultures, and societies. This enables us to use cultural sources to guide us in interacting wisely in our families, or to make sure that we choose dependable beliefs to inspire our endeavors. In addition, freeing ourselves from social class expectations or societies' ethnocentrism, inevitably involves making new cultural choices. For example, when we opt to go in directions that better our societies, we increase both our gender fulfillment and our social intelligence.

Social intelligence heightens our awareness of cultural choices, and helps us to appreciate the complexities and power of our cultural resources. For example, our life outcomes are markedly different when we prioritize equality rather than competitiveness in our everyday activities. More especially, our gender fulfillment increases when we accept particular clusters of values as our own, such as values in religions, sciences, arts, or education. Thus, social intelligence helps us to stay in charge of our destinies through making more enlightened value choices, which strengthens our gender fulfillment.

One of the preconditions of making wise value choices, which motivate us to accomplish our preferred gender goals effectively, is to give priority to the values of autonomy and independence. For example, we need to be relatively free to choose values which enhance our gender identities, so that we see the broader pictures of our lives. Consequently, we are selective in making decisions and commitments that yield both meaning and fulfillment to our genders.

Sizing up our gendered social situations is not easy. For example, all too frequently we are so set in our ways that we close ourselves off from possibilities that could make us more fulfilled. We frequently do not see what is already in our cultures as value choices. However, when our starting point is our genders, and our valued resources are our national and international cultures, we are more likely to achieve gender fulfillment than if we consider ourselves to be isolated individuals without resources.

Gender fulfillment results from expressing male and female dimensions of genders, sexualities, and sexual orientations, as well as interests that are not directly related to genders. Social intelligence gives us the broadest views of who we are, so that issues about our gender fulfillment become objective and universal rather than narrow and parochial. Thus, social intelligence encourages us to use social justice ideals, which maintain our focus on living fully both within and outside our personal milieus.

VI. Societies and Gender

Societies are the fifth major social influence of social intelligence to shed light on how we identify and act according to our genders. Therefore, in order to understand our genders and to be more effective in our gendered actions, we need to consider how societies and groups of societies affect our gender choices, in addition to how families, beliefs, social classes, and cultures influence who we are and what we do.

We do not live in vacuums in our complex social worlds. Social intelligence shows us that we strengthen our immunity to the push and pull of the five major social influences of families, beliefs, social classes, cultures, and societies by examining how we operate—individually and socially—in relation to families, beliefs, social classes, cultures, and societies.

We also need to assess whatever we discover to be our habitual styles of interacting with families, beliefs, social classes, cultures, and societies, so that we can change what we do in order to achieve our preferred goals more effectively. For example, when we examine how we interact with our societies as historical beings, we may decide to become more enlightened or more active in broad social concerns. This increases our capacities to reach our goals as historical actors, who address significant social issues like gender inequalities.

Sometimes we make gender choices directly from examining the extent to which our learned genders hold us back from what we want to accomplish, rather than launch us into ever-increasing spheres of social interactions and social significance. If we associate being passive with being a woman, for example, this pattern of behavior predictably hinders the effectiveness of communications between different genders, as well as our attainment of independent goals. In this situation, especially if we are women, we may become more socially intelligent by deliberately choosing to nurture aggressive or assertive values, in order to strengthen our motivation and focus while reducing gender inequalities.

Societies show some of their power over genders when we examine different priorities expressed by patriotic values, or historical trends in gender behavior. For example, when societies are warlike, there are often more extreme differences between expectations for women and men. However, because gender equality in societies increased in recent decades, there is also more fluidity and flexibility in defining genders in similar ways. Whatever aspects of societal influences we choose to consider, in assessing the impacts societies and histories have on genders, we necessarily conclude that societies strongly affect how populations define and live their genders.

When we pose questions about how to use social intelligence to change our genders and societies, we find that even making slight modifications in seeing ourselves in societies influences our life outcomes and aptitudes for reaching constructive social goals. For example, social intelligence shows us that our actions flow from our understanding of societies, as well as from recognizing the importance of families, beliefs, social classes, and cultures. This means that we must pay close attention to what our nations and global communities need, with respect to our genders and accomplishments.

For some, understanding our evolutionary origins is an important aspect of societies, because evolution addresses concerns about the nature of human nature as well as critical gender issues. To the extent that we see evolutionary forces as strong or dominant in social change, for example, our answers to questions about how to modify our genders are different from those who do not consider evolution to be a primary influence in societies. In any event, how we go about changing our genders or sexualities should optimally include considerations about societies as well as families, beliefs, social classes, and cultures.

VI. Societies and Gender

Perspectives about societies broaden our socially intelligent views of social realities, so that we define our genders and sexualities more realistically and more objectively. Broad socially intelligent perspectives on societies also put our sexual orientation concerns in context, so that we make more informed gender choices, assume more strategic gender responsibilities, and achieve greater gender fulfillment. We are who we are, and we are more likely to become who we want to be, when we assess our genders through social intelligence and societies, as well as serve the common good or social justice for our societies and the world.

Gender Defined

Technically, much of what we conventionally define as genders is described and explained in terms of contrasting gender roles, which are often viewed and understood in societal contexts. For example, historically most societies have prescribed dichotomies or polar opposites for separate gender roles, which reflect largely unequal distributions of power and prestige for women and men. Furthermore, these frequently complementary gender roles tend to reinforce patterns in basic divisions of labor among men and women, which have been held over long periods of time. Consequently, traditional societal gender roles often reinforce arbitrary and limited role expectations for both women and men.

Social intelligence requires us to question the assumptions we make about gender roles in societies, because gender roles often sustain the status quo of societies in conservative or traditional ways. Social intelligence clarifies how gender roles can be changed, or at least neutralized, especially in their negative impacts on realizing the potentials of both women and men. Therefore, even though examining the many influences of societies on gender definitions is a socially intelligent strategy, this must involve much more than focusing solely on gender roles per se.

Because societal patterns of gender behavior enliven historical perspectives on gender definitions, social intelligence deepens our understanding of gender. For example, when we see historical variations of genders in different societies, together with varied national priorities in relation to genders, we realize not only that our own societies' definitions of gender are limited, but also that they are distorted by vested interests which influence the relative opportunities of women and men.

In order to gain objectivity about our gendered life choices and gendered life chances, we need to use social intelligence to make thoughtful comparisons among societies, as well as to comprehend the vastness of the gendered consequences of globalization. We live in circumstances that make us not as geographically distant from each other as in the past—largely due to technologies of modern travel and communication—so we need to adapt to globalization directly, rather than ignore its contrasts and contradictions, if we are to survive and be fulfilled.

We all benefit from creating broad definitions of gender through knowledge about societal and world perspectives. We cannot risk restricting our expectations for men and women artificially or unnecessarily if we want to benefit from already-existing wide ranges of human talents, particularly if we aspire to deal efficiently with the complex and powerful demands of our national and international communities. Gender is a force to be used rather than denied or wasted, and social intelligence guides us to create constructive ways to employ this powerful resource, if only due to the seriousness of current worldwide crises and needs.

One way out of some of these overwhelming dilemmas is to be deliberately cautious in defining genders. For example, we desperately need to raise children who respect each other and their genders. Now is not the time to fall back on repetitions of traditional gender roles, but rather to make it possible for gender variations and significant nuances in gender differences to coexist peacefully. We cannot afford to lose any of the creative and purposeful energies of genders, by reacting destructively to new gender developments. Rather, we must focus on cultivating considerable flexibility in our responsiveness to genders. This means that we will welcome all to our tables, so that we can share gender resources rather than declare preferences for particular kinds of womanhood or manhood.

VI. Societies and Gender

The broadest perspectives of societies help us to practice this quality of reflection, as well as enhance our capacities to be objective. Similarly, social intelligence heightens our awareness of how we can take the next steps to accomplish our shared responsible goals of building better worlds for tomorrow. Only when we have realized the importance of broadening, rather than narrowing, our definitions of genders can we proceed to embrace significant differences in sexualities, sexual orientations, gender responsibilities, and gender fulfillment.

Defining genders carefully is important to both individuals and societies, because these definitions are bases for our lived gender identities. We absorb into the deepest levels of our being what we consider to be the particular characteristics of genders that express who we are most accurately. Thus our senses of self are intimately tied to our gender identities, as well as to our definitions of responsibilities as socially intelligent human beings.

Gender and Sexuality

Societies are actors in history because they are political units that represent whole populations. The historical dimensions of societies reflect the dominant ways in which populations organize themselves through time, around continuing social issues such as genders and sexualities. However, some of the patterns in genders and sexualities are characterized by cycles as well as by linear history. Therefore, we cannot easily predict, from social facts about societies, what particular trends in genders and sexualities are now or will be in the future.

Social intelligence shows us advantages from cultivating our broadest views of genders and sexualities in societal perspectives. For example, we become aware of the major social influence of societies on our individual and social behavior: we are who we are because we were oriented to use our genders and sexualities in particular ways, and because we model our gender behavior in relation to what other people do—especially those who are in the same social classes, or who have received similar education.

Even though some biological and physiological research suggests that we may have very few choices in genders and sexualities, we are predominantly social beings, and can decide how to express our genders and sexualities in meaningful ways. It is significant that our given genders and sexualities may be channeled into a wide variety of individual and social behaviors, so that we are ultimately in charge of being at least more or less responsible in our gendered, sexual actions.

Social intelligence shows us that we can separate our thinking about genders and sexualities, so that we are not deterministic in believing that because we are a specific gender we must act in particular sexual ways. Our genders and sexualities do not predetermine our behavior. We have wide ranges of possibilities to choose from in expressing our sexualities, whether we are women or men. Using social intelligence to increase our freedom of choice is an important result of becoming more socially intelligent, especially because social intelligence serves us as a reliable guide for conducting our day-to-day business and acting responsibly.

We become socially intelligent historical actors only when we see gender and sexuality connections as individuals in families, communities, and societies. Cultivating broad perspectives to view our actions in societies makes us more socially intelligent, because we can then be more committed to initiating broad social changes that increase the common good and social justice. In this way, social intelligence provides us with valuable goals that transcend improving our families and clarifying personal patterns of behavior.

Seeing societies for what they are frees us from being more or less trapped by our interpersonal lives in families and communities. For example, societies allow us to see our broader purposes more clearly and more meaningfully, so that we then drop some of our self interests in order to work toward improving the common good and social justice. We recognize that self interests usually cannot save our societies, and that in order to be sure of building the common good and social justice today for tomorrow, we must consider the goals of all our daily decisions, including those related to our genders and sexualities.

National and international social movements, such as feminism and gay rights, have taught us that individual and social rights are hard won, and that we must be ever-vigilant about genders and sexualities. Special interest groups that represent particular genders and sexualities are often strong, and may resist social changes that require a broader social acceptance of varied genders and sexualities. However, in the long run, we all need to move toward increasing gender and sexual diversity, in order to ensure world peace, as well as individual and social fulfillment.

Merely thinking about significant social issues, such as genders and sexualities, helps us to both survive and be fulfilled. Social intelligence principles guide us to accomplish goals that improve the quality of life in our societies, only after we have come to grips with the seriousness of those gender and sexuality social issues that pervade our societies. Using broad societal perspectives is essential for improving societies, and we know we are on our way to achieve our socially intelligent goals when we find that our genders and sexualities are constructive resources.

Gender and Sexual Orientation

Societies are also a useful social intelligence perspective from which to understand genders and sexual orientations. For example, we size up current social issues about genders and sexual orientations more accurately, when we compare historical perspectives on how our own societies and other societies have restricted gender behaviors, sexualities, and sexual orientations over the years. In many respects, societies share common concerns that genders, sexualities, and sexual orientations should be regulated in some way, so that societies maintain stability through time.

Another reason for societies to control their populations—with respect to genders, sexualities, and sexual orientations—is so that appropriate rates of procreation can be produced to replace recently deceased members of our populations. For example, we need to sustain satisfactory rates of population growth due to the fertility that results more directly from widespread behaviors around genders, sexualities, and sexual orientations. Unless populations sustain heterosexuality to an adequate extent, their members are not replaced as satisfactorily and as smoothly as possible.

Thus, genders and sexual orientations may be significant catalysts in essentially enhancing or blocking the smooth functioning of societies themselves. This is an important reason why societies may initially feel threatened by homosexual behavior rather than heterosexual behavior. For example, at gut levels we often believe that homosexual behavior can possibly lead relatively quickly to declines in rigorous population growth, while heterosexual behavior more obviously supports populations as we know them. However, civilizations are built on very complex humane and social considerations. Therefore, our reactions of fear and deprivation should not dominate our best efforts and intentions to build our preferred societies for the future, where the sexual freedom of all is protected.

Social intelligence makes us soon see that in addition to these basic issues about the reproductive survival of societies, societies need to consider social justice concerns related to homosexuality and heterosexuality. Because each of us depends on our societies for survival, we have to ensure optimal social conditions for all, rather than simply for majorities in our societies. For example, social intelligence shows us a variety of practical ways to undertake responsible universal approaches to ensuring freedom throughout society, which require us to work together cooperatively and productively.

When such supportive societal conditions of concern and equality exist, we are more easily able to honor each other sufficiently freely in terms of our genders and sexual orientations. However, at no point do we need everyone in a single society to conform to the same or similar standards of gender and sexual orientation. Rather, we must find new ways to cooperate with each other in order to build and maintain more flexible and more just societies. We are inspired to work toward increasing the common good through genders and sexual orientations, for example, when we see how much societies need firm foundations in order to function well.

Positive conditions for nurturing gender and sexual diversity gradually win freedom, dignity, and social honor. Challenging, hiding, or denying contrasts in gender and sexual orientations become less necessary, and more people start to contribute to increasing the common good. These social conditions develop sufficient social trust for us to be who we really are, by living more openly and more cooperatively than before.

The significance of establishing social conditions of freedom throughout our societies is not obvious, unless we continue to consider the broadest social perspectives of our societies. For example, our particular social situations are understood more fully when we assess legal systems and their impacts on the quality of life of whole populations, especially with regard to genders and sexual orientations. Constancy in using this breadth of perspective helps us to build optimal societies today for the future.

We deliberately use future views of what our societies could be like, in order to create meaningful contexts for our efforts to increase the common good and social justice through societies, genders, and sexual orientations. For example, we realize that we are making social changes for the next generations as well as our own, when we look ahead carefully to the future. Only in this way can we take full advantage of our many gender choices, live responsibly, and achieve fulfillment through our genders and sexual orientations.

Gender Choices

Societies inevitably provide us with many complex views of ourselves and possibilities for individual and social actions. When we are focused on genders, sexualities, and sexual orientations, the expansiveness and breadth of societal perspectives shed light on choices and opportunities that we were not aware of previously. Therefore, when we consider our gendered lives more closely, and in relation to the five major social influences of families, beliefs, social classes, cultures, and societies, we increase our social intelligence and at the same time open up considerably more practical options for genders. We begin to see our way out of the suffocating restrictions that limited our choices in the past.

Taking advantage of new ranges of societal choices about gender ultimately directs us toward individual and social issues about gender responsibilities and fulfillment. For example, we are responsible when we do our best to ensure that no stones are left unturned, and that we have acted on state of the art social facts about genders in whatever we choose to do. Our goals usually reflect some of the ways in which we feel trapped or liberated in our gendered lives, because we aspire to make the world a better place for all, rather than maintain the status quo of vested interests, exploitation, and oppression.

Educating ourselves about how people express their genders in different societies is a strategic way to take advantage of the increased gender options we find in contemporary societies. By exploring and comparing the histories of different societies, we deepen our understanding of progressive or regressive gender choices, especially in relation to the passage of time, and the impacts of increased education for the masses in modern societies. Even though many people are critical of media influences on genders and sexual orientations, for example, some of our most destructive taboos of silence about genders and sexual orientations have been broken or modified through mass communications in contemporary societies. For example, we now sense that we are discovering ways out of the many impasses that members of past generations had left virtually untouched.

Gender choices that have considerable impacts on life outcomes importantly include value choices. These are not so much moral choices of right over wrong, but rather choices that seem to be the most practical options we can take to reach our socially intelligent goals of increasing the common good and social justice for all. When we see that we have these options in many varied social situations, we work together cooperatively and effectively to create better futures from our current restrictive situations.

VI. Societies and Gender

We pay particular attention to gender choices for people of all ages, because it is never too late to start life over by using new sets of gender value choices. For example, we can change our social commitments in relatively short periods of time if we wish to do so. Furthermore, however powerful and complex the five major social influences of families, beliefs, social classes, cultures, and societies are, we can relate to them differently immediately, so that we avoid continuing to be trapped or victimized by their power and effects.

In addition, we need to recognize the choices that young adults make, as well as the choices we give our children. Young people are decision-makers for the next generations, and the quality of life in populations ultimately depends on their leadership and imagination. It is crucial that deep understanding and continuing commitments to resolve gender issues are passed on through the generations. However, we can only accomplish this deliberately, because continuities in learning and expressing equity among genders do not occur automatically. We must carve out improved futures now, in order to protect us from traditions that too frequently overtake our best individual and social intentions to create more liberated futures.

Social intelligence prepares us all to be sufficiently watchful and knowledgeable in making enlightened gender choices. Social intelligence does not maintain the status quo or vested interests. Rather, we learn from societies and give back to societies, because our well-being depends on others as well as ourselves. For example, we teach children and young adults about improved possibilities, because we need them to carry on our work of creating and maintaining positive gender choices for the future.

Gender Responsibilities

Gender responsibilities emerge as we become more socially intelligent. Becoming more socially intelligent means that we are aware of what it takes to be responsible, and how this relates to our genders. For example, it is virtually impossible to assume some important gender responsibilities, unless we have a mature and full understanding of what genders mean, how we define genders, how we deal with gendered sexualities and sexual orientations, and how we make gender choices.

We also become more responsible when we define our worlds in broader terms than our own hand to mouth survival. We need to have sufficient resources to be able to establish a certain degree of detachment or objectivity about our social situations, so that we can see what it is that we want to accomplish in relation to our genders. When we use societies as broad socially intelligent perspectives on genders, we consider our lives in more meaningful contexts, and are more selective in choosing and assuming individual and social responsibilities.

An important aspect of becoming socially intelligent is to question what we take for granted, and what others expect of us. Understanding societies and genders helps us to articulate our gender responsibilities, and we pay attention to conventional gender expectations for different ages and circumstances. With these starting points, we assess more astutely whether we want to make conventional gender commitments, especially when we juxtapose these with our strongest preferences for achieving our unique gender commitments and goals.

Whittling down the number of our chosen gender responsibilities gives us increased personal, professional, and political freedom, as well as allows us to make deeper commitments to particular gender responsibilities. We decide to assume only those responsibilities that we care about the most, so that we become more authentic historical actors who make responsible gender changes.

When we assume gender responsibilities in socially intelligent ways, we prioritize our gender goals and focus our gendered efforts on them. We are more productive when we do not disperse our energies too much among different goals, and aim to enhance rather than diminish our efforts. We continue to consider the societal dimensions of our gendered responsibilities, so that we see more clearly how much we need others in order to work responsibly toward our gendered goals.

VI. Societies and Gender

Socially intelligent societal perspectives confirm that our gender responsibilities gradually achieve more gender equality in all societies. Thinking in terms of whole societies enables us to look beyond gendered vested interests, as does our nurturing of broad socially intelligent values such as equality, inclusiveness, diversity, cooperation, and openness in our gender identities, sexualities, and sexual orientations. Thinking more universally empowers us to consider gender responsibilities in international communities, so that we intervene in global processes when needed.

Social intelligence is founded on having a sound working knowledge of societies. Only when we cultivate socially intelligent vantage points, from which to understand and assess gender responsibilities, can we select our gendered priorities and act effectively toward increasing the common good and social justice.

We may also choose to follow leads from our own specific talents and gifts, whatever these skills may be, so that we contribute indirectly to increasing the common good and social justice for genders. For example, social intelligence may allow us to become better artists and scientists, than if we focus solely on assuming specific gendered responsibilities. Thus, although we may not strive to improve opportunities for people of different genders and sexualities, when we live fully as gendered beings who are artists or scientists, we automatically inspire others by expressing our genders and contributing to societies as artists or scientists.

In order to sort out our priorities, in terms of deciding what our responsibilities are, it is important to recall that social intelligence does not require us to be over-responsible for ourselves or others, but rather to be balanced in assuming responsibilities for our genders, sexualities, and sexual orientations. Existentially, we need to be fulfilled—as well as to survive—whenever possible. However, in many respects this ultimately means that we should honor others in some of the same ways in which we would like to be recognized and respected, as we go about our lives each day. Furthermore, social intelligence suggests that our social justice value choices of equality, inclusiveness, diversity, cooperation, and openness will clear the way for our constructive actions and goals, especially in times of ambiguity and anguish.

Gender Fulfillment

Societies are a significant fifth strand of social intelligence, and they guide us to be more comprehensive in our understanding of what gender fulfillment is. For example, societies compel us to see the broader pictures of our genders and gender fulfillment, so that we make more meaningful assessments in deciding what our gender choices should be. Furthermore, when we see ourselves in societal contexts, we broaden our concerns for the well-being of others, rather than stay focused on individual or family concerns.

Gender fulfillment derives from understanding genders in societies, and from expressing our genders constructively in this broad context. For example, the more we live our genders responsibly, the more we are fulfilled by accomplishing specific gender goals. Gender fulfillment flows from knowing our gender capacities, selecting meaningful gendered goals, and accomplishing our chosen objectives. One of our existential challenges is to plan our lives deliberately, so that we give ourselves chances to succeed in creating the kinds of lives we really want to live. Unless we undertake this responsibility, we will not achieve our preferred goals, and we will not gain the satisfaction and fulfillment we yearn.

We also need to transcend narrow definitions of our genders in order to achieve gender fulfillment. For example, we know that our gendered goals are right for us when we understand them in the context of our societies, and when we establish priorities to accomplish them. Furthermore, when we recognize the social fact of conventional gender limitations for both women and men, we see that we may focus our efforts best by not being gender specific in formulating our goals.

Becoming more socially intelligent includes viewing our lives from societies' perspectives. For example, we understand our gender challenges more fully when we consider ourselves as historical actors. We no longer see ourselves only as gendered beings in the here and now, but rather participate in historical processes that show us both our gendered roots of the past, and our gendered aspirations for the present and future. Furthermore, the broad perspectives of societies' histories give us special vantage points from which to assess our missions as historical actors.

Our understanding of ourselves deepens when we live more fully as historical actors. Transcendental goals increase our senses of purpose, as well as possibilities for being fulfilled through our gendered intentions and actions. New social realities dominate our concerns, and we are more fulfilled through our appropriate actions. We no longer merely react, as we meet our daily individual and family needs, when we consider ourselves as historical actors. Recognizing the inherent precariousness of social realities motivates us to change societies in ways that we may have previously thought impossible.

Our focuses shift when we live more fully as historical actors, partly because we work more cooperatively with others when we increase our social intelligence. Understanding that we cannot reach our goals effectively through our own isolated efforts, moves us to find like-minded others with whom to cooperate, so that we make shared commitments to reach our goals. Thus, we accomplish more of our common good agenda cooperatively, than through random individual efforts.

Social intelligence shows us that gender fulfillment occurs when we use our know-how about societies to discover meaningful goals to motivate us, as well as significant others with whom to work. We inspire each other when we see our societies as arenas of change, which are impacted by collective efforts. Further, we recognize that increasing gender equity in one sphere of society, such as education, creates waves of change in social conditions throughout societies. When we learn how to experience our genders differently, we make new value choices, and are more productive in reforming or transforming our societies.

Considering genders in our societies, as well as possibilities for changing gendered patterns of behavior, challenges us to continue to increase our social intelligence. This gives us reliable, meaningful guidance on how to achieve a greater common good or social justice in societies and the global community. Using social intelligence to work in these directions increases our accomplishments and yields greater gender fulfillment, which motivate us to sustain our efforts in the long run. In fact, as long as we ensure that we are heading in our preferred directions, satisfaction and fulfillment will accompany our efforts.

Social Intelligence
Guides Gender

VII. Objectivity and Gender

Social intelligence increases our objectivity about ourselves, our situations, and our genders. When we are objective, or less emotionally bound to our day-to-day expectations and routines, we see more of our options for alternative action in any given set of social circumstances. In this respect, objectivity ultimately increases the qualities of our life chances, because we are freer to advance in new directions that are often ultimately more rewarding than those which are merely familiar, or parts of our daily routines. For example, we may decide to make gender a central priority in sizing up our situations and taking action.

Being objective about our genders, sexualities, and sexual orientations involves a basic shift in our thinking and actions. For example, we put our original conditioning to one side— even only temporarily—so that we can see broader horizons of possibilities and choices for ourselves and others. We no longer go with the flow of the endless repetitions of what we have done before, but rather take a deep breath to give us courage, so that we get on with our lives relatively fearlessly in different ways. This includes prioritizing gender issues in our decision-making and commitments, as well as through our socially intelligent actions.

Social intelligence gives us new ways to think, to assess social conditions, and to respond to our day-by-day situations. Consequently, we are ready and more capable in connecting what goes on in our personal lives to the broad social influences in globalization. For example, we see how our current genders, sexualities, and sexual orientations are impacted by the five major social influences of families, beliefs, social classes, cultures, and societies. Furthermore, in addition to heightening our awareness about existing conditions, we commit ourselves to living according to social intelligence principles.

Becoming more objective about how gender, sexuality, and sexual orientation affect some of the most significant social aspects of our lives, helps us to establish new priorities. For example, we use objectivity to reflect about what is most pressing in our current gender and sexuality situations. Being socially intelligent does not mean that we miss out on deep aspects of living, but rather that we make ourselves more capable of going forward productively, in order to meet our preferred goals.

When we define who we are through socially intelligent ways of considering our genders, sexualities, and sexual orientations, our actions become more meaningful to us and to others. For example, we may assume more missions as historical actors, or pursue social justice goals, which directly increase the common good for gender concerns. We also stay aware of our emotional connectedness to others, and give serious thought to how we are contributing to history, by building on some of our triumphs and mistakes of the past.

Overall, we use social intelligence to continuously review our gender choices, and at the same time strengthen our commitments to particular gender responsibilities. This means that we are more awake each day, and achieve more satisfactory gender fulfillment in whatever we decide to do. Above all we strive for objectivity so that we can maintain broad perspectives in our understanding of genders, sexualities, and sexual orientations, and be prepared to choose new options to deal with social justice and gender concerns. Even in coping with our day-to-day needs, social intelligence clarifies our value choices, so that we stay focused on our preferred goals.

This path of increased objectivity helps us to achieve our dreams. However, only when we let go of conventional expectations about genders, sexualities, and sexual orientations can we proceed wholeheartedly in these new directions. Our enthusiasm for improved social options motivates us to use social intelligence to develop worthwhile goals for all, so we can cooperate more effectively in these ventures.

Being more objective loosens the grip of our limited expectations about individual and social possibilities. However, when we relax our hold on our present social circumstances, we become more realistic—and even more idealistic—about how to proceed in dealing with ongoing social conditions in local, national, and international arenas. Our objectivity is an ongoing major accomplishment, which connects us to both narrow and broad dimensions of our lived realities, so that we are well-prepared to improve social circumstances in the present for the future.

Gender Defined

We define our genders and gender identities according to the meanings we associate with our gender choices. For example, if we understand genders to be a simple dichotomy between conventional, mainstream male and female characteristics, we will identify with whichever of these two basic choices we find more congenial. However, if we understand genders to be more complex than this, with many overlapping interests and talents among men and women, we will be more cautious about how we define and construct our genders. Objectivity and flexibility may guide our definitions of some of these nuances, especially where overlapping characteristics are considered to be female or male.

By encouraging us to maintain objectivity, social intelligence educates us about the varied ways in which genders are defined. For example, social intelligence is based on social facts about genders in contrasting cultures and different time periods. This increases possibilities for defining genders and gender identities. Furthermore, social intelligence encourages us to explore and try to understand these varied social facts, so that we are surer of our commitments to the particular characteristics we choose to associate with being women or men.

In this way social intelligence consistently moves us toward appreciating the power and complexities of genders, rather than stops at superficial interpretations of what it means to be a woman or a man. For example, we see that we need to become whole persons if we are to live fully in modern societies, and that objectivity helps us to make more mature choices about which values will motivate us to achieve our gendered goals and ideals.

Because gender characteristics differ so markedly, we need not replicate any particular model of being male or female. In order to be authentic in our selections, we might choose to define our genders according to our experiences with the five major social influences of families, beliefs, social classes, cultures, and societies, which anchor us meaningfully in ongoing social situations and ventures. Similarly, when we define genders in ways that help us to accomplish our most cherished goals, we are more likely to bring our strengths to bear constructively on others.

Considering the influence of genders in our families makes us realize how much our subjective awareness of genders derives from personal experiences of gender that we encountered when we were young. Thus, we increase our objectivity through practicing social intelligence as we find broader and deeper sources of gender inspiration. When these gender identities diverge from our families' expectations, we cultivate new patterns of gender exchanges in our families.

Similarly, we need to become more objective about the gender beliefs we inherited from our families, schools, communities, and societies. We do this by researching new sources of gender beliefs throughout the world, which guide our definitions of genders more authentically. For example, we accept beliefs about genders that resonate with our own preferences and ideals, rather than those which merely replicate what we have done in the past.

Social intelligence also educates us about how to define our genders according to social classes. Loyalties to social classes, or aspirations to join particular social classes, usually move us to make limited decisions about genders and our daily life. We use the objectivity of social intelligence to critically assess our restricted visions of social class gender possibilities, so that we free ourselves from restrictions and stereotypes in defining our identities.

Our needs to be objective turn us back to our cultures, which are other major sources of alternative gender definitions and identities. Cultural symbols and meanings provide us with new dimensions of genders, which consistently give us broad reference points for constructing our genders. For example, we make wiser value choices about genders when we appreciate how objectivity expands our cultural options for defining genders.

The fifth dimension of social intelligence, that affects our objectivity and gender identities, is our awareness of gender in societies throughout the world. We benefit from assessing the extent to which societies' definitions of genders create historical changes, for example, and how we can participate in our societies more fully by redefining genders. When we are objective historical actors, we use our gender identities to work cooperatively with others, so that we make the most effective changes in the common good.

Gender and Sexuality

Just as increasing objectivity, through developing our social intelligence, helps us to be more deliberate in defining our genders, we also use objectivity to recognize and practice our sexualities. For example, being objective strengthens our capacities to assess specifically how families, beliefs, social classes, cultures, and societies define our life chances, genders, and sexualities. What are the governing social facts in these major social influences? What are the odds of being able to ask the most critical questions about the social forces that evoke such strong emotions? Why does it matter that we try to be rational about our options rather than reactive?

We discover that we gain freedom when we are more objective about what our sexualities require, so that we thrive and sustain our efforts to improve our lives and achieve our goals more effectively. Being objective helps us to persist in our efforts to make gender changes over the long haul. For these reasons we choose to let social intelligence and objectivity guide us as much as possible in our everyday decision-making. We learn more from others, and teach social intelligence skills more clearly, when we are objective.

Just as being objective about our individual and social behavior, as well as our social situations, increases our options in employing our sexualities, we can choose to be objective about our personal and social sexualities. For example, objectivity helps us to acknowledge the power and complexities of sexualities in families, beliefs, social classes, cultures, and societies, so that we strengthen our social bonds and commitments.

Our non-rational resistance to objectivity derives largely from patterns of interaction and interdependence in our families. From being infants, we tend to be enmeshed in strong emotional and social influences, which condition us to have particular sexualities. For example, if we were raised to be traditional women and men, we usually develop many of the conventional characteristics of polarized sexualities. Although we can neutralize, to some extent, families' pressures which support such traditional sexual practices, we often return to our initial sexualities when we are stressed or disoriented about our own life purposes.

Social intelligence shows us that these emotional foundations of our being are expressed through our everyday beliefs, as well as through clusters of beliefs such as family religions or relatives' politics. However, because we are motivated and fueled by our beliefs, we need to be more objective about them, if we are to direct our decisions and commitments to express our sexualities constructively. Only when we use social intelligence to deliberately choose our preferred beliefs more objectively, can we create better worlds for all.

A third strand of social intelligence is based on our more objective understanding of how social classes influence our sexual practices. As we mature through developing social intelligence, we accept the social fact that our sexualities are not entirely personal and private aspects of our intimate lives as we had previously thought. For example, when we are more objective about who we are, we see that even our sexualities are patterned according to some social class considerations, and that our sexual practices may be integral parts of our strivings for upward social mobility. Our objectivity and social intelligence help us to be more aware of these tendencies, which gives us sufficient freedom and autonomy to modify how we stay connected to our genders and sexualities.

Social intelligence also uses cultures to strengthen our objectivity. For example, we become more objective when we refresh our ideas about our sexualities, as well as our knowledge of different options in expressing our sexualities, by immersing ourselves in both familiar and contrasting cultures. Our cultural bases of social intelligence inspire us to innovate in our sexual practices wherever necessary, so that we can relate more meaningfully to the flow of social changes in our cultures. Therefore, our sexualities and objectivity are partly cultural expressions, which inspire us to accomplish our preferred goals for the common good and social justice more fully.

Societies are the fifth major social influence that affects our objectivity and our lives. We gain objectivity when we recognize and understand more fully how our sexualities are expressed in national and global societal contexts. For example, social intelligence guides us to be historical actors, but we need to be ever vigilant about how our sexualities sustain our capacities to increase the common good and social justice. We cannot compartmentalize our actions so that they merely express particular genders or sexualities, if we are to accomplish more objective universal goals as historical actors.

Gender and Sexual Orientation

Our socially intelligent awareness of gender and objectivity includes considering relationships between our genders and sexual orientations. For example, we cannot deny or exclude the fact that sexual orientations have become increasingly important in how people understand their genders in modern societies. Nor can we deny or exclude the fact that in general, mainstream society usually tolerates differences in sexual orientations reluctantly, rather than embraces them as essential characteristics of human diversity.

In these respects, deepening our understanding of objectivity in social intelligence, and how objectivity affects our experiences of connections between genders and sexual orientations, opens up possibilities for expression rather than imposes further restrictions. For example, we deal with others' reactions of prejudice and discrimination more effectively when we are objective about understanding this problematic behavior. Realizing how people's homosexual orientations upset heterosexual others gives us a head start for holding our ground in cultivating and sustaining diversity in sexual orientations.

We become more objective about sexual orientations, and their links to our genders, when we trace their impacts in the five major social influences of families, beliefs, social classes, cultures, and societies. Examining sexual orientations in these significant social contexts makes us more knowledgeable about how we experience our own sexual orientations, and how much we conform to social standards in expressing our sexual orientations. Ultimately, being more objective about ourselves loosens the hold that the five major social influences have over our behavior, and gives us more freedom to carve out new ways to deal with our sexual orientations and genders.

First, knowing the power of family influences on our sexual orientations explains how deeply ingrained our sexual orientations are, due to the impacts of significant others' views on our sexual orientations. For example, many families have no direct experiences of relatives' lesbian or gay sexual orientations, or they may resist openness to homosexuality issues. Being more objective about the social significance of sexual orientation labels, as well as the gender implications of sexual orientations, helps us to deal with these strong prejudices and discrimination. However, we need to cultivate objectivity, in order to move beyond our limited experiences of dealing with genders and sexual orientations. This allows us to be socially intelligent in more of our our actions and commitments.

Second, the power of beliefs on our sexual orientations explains how others' understanding of sexual orientations affects our world views in relating to those who have either like or unlike beliefs. Although it is usually easier to cooperate with people who are likeminded, being in the real world also requires us to have sufficient objectivity to communicate and work with those who have contrasting beliefs. Social intelligence helps us to accomplish this, by directing us to work with both those who share our beliefs and those who do not. When we are more objective, we more easily agree on goals, purposes, and directions, or decide to reach our goals by taking different paths.

A third major social influence in how we understand sexual orientations is social classes. Only when we are sufficiently objective to set aside complex and powerful social class pressures to be socially mobile, or to protect our own social class interests, are we sufficiently free to sustain objectivity by taking socially intelligent actions. For example, we deliberately nurture objectivity, so that we express our sexual orientations more forthrightly, and with consideration for others—especially those who have contrasting sexual orientations.

Our needs to be objective about sexual orientations and genders drive us to more fully understand rich varieties of humankind through our cultures, the fourth major social influence of social intelligence. We cannot easily decide to be objective, or to avail ourselves of cultural choices, unless we learn more about our cultures and the options that cultural knowledge provides about sexual orientations and genders. We turn to cultures to see how people with different sexual orientations express themselves through their genders, for example, so that we can make more enlightened choices in our own behavior.

The fifth major social influence that affects who we are in relation to our sexual orientations and genders is societies. Societies and history necessarily enhance our objectivity because of their broad perspectives. For example, we understand our sexual orientations and genders more fully when we compare our sexual orientations and genders with those experienced by other societies. We also understand the pressures of sexual orientations and genders more adequately when we examine their historical trends in different societies. These assessments strengthen our objectivity because they give us more social facts to consider, in making decisions and commitments about our own complex, powerful societies.

Gender Choices

In order to be sure that we are living according to principles of social intelligence, whereby we make the most of the gender choices we have available to us, we must continue to cultivate our capacities to be objective, as well as persevere in identifying social intelligence principles in our families, beliefs, social classes, cultures, and societies. Social intelligence principles are built on the social facts we acknowledge and use in relation to the five major social influences of families, beliefs, social classes, cultures, and societies. Furthermore, our objectivity and freedom from restrictive social influences depend on the reliability of our knowledge of families, beliefs, social classes, cultures, and societies.

Gender choices include options about our sexualities and sexual orientations. Although it is clear that our gender choices are more than our sexualities and sexual orientations, we cannot afford to deny the importance of the physiological foundations of our genders. Social intelligence emphasizes the social aspects of how we acquire and continue to construct our genders, because then we can change at least some aspects of our learned gender behavior, in order to increase freedom in others' lives as well as our own.

Families are the most intense emotional sources of our gender conditioning, in part because we receive family members' thoughts and feelings about gender issues when we are embryos and during the most impressionable years of our earliest personal development and maturation. Moreover, our socialization results from repeated patterns of interaction through different generations in our families, which are strong and powerful influences in their own right. In order to gain more control over our gender choices, however, we must establish ourselves more firmly in our families and other social groups by being more objective. This allows us to get more in charge of our gender choices, rather than furthers our passivity about families' messages and examples about what gender is or should be in our lives.

Beliefs are also foundations of our genders, often through our families. However, beliefs frequently result from social exchanges in our schools, religions, communities, peer groups, and friendship networks. Exploring these varied social sources of our beliefs about genders changes the impacts of our gender socialization, so that we more easily create gender identities that we truly choose: social intelligence and increased objectivity allow us to be more selective about which beliefs we nurture; and we see what our real options are, choose what beliefs we need, and construct our genders today for the future.

A third aspect of social intelligence, which enables us to be freer in our gender choices, is the major social influence of social classes. Our awareness of the significance of social classes, and their impacts on our gendered socialization and current gender choices, guides us toward increased objectivity. Both social intelligence and objectivity show us that we are stronger when we reduce the impacts of conventional social classes based on genders, sexualities, sexual orientations, material resources, occupation, race, ethnicity, education, and ablebodiedness.

Cultures are another important aspect of social intelligence. We clarify their impacts by reviewing cultural choices in our gender conditioning. When we expand our gender choices, we become more objective about ourselves and our cultural choices. For example, if we were raised to be members of particular religions when we were young, this does not necessarily mean that we must stay in these religions for the rest of our lives. Making more objective cultural decisions and commitments today frees us from some of the restrictive religious and gender conditioning that we experienced during earlier stages of our development.

The fifth aspect of social intelligence that historically restricted our gender choices is how societies impact our thinking and acting.

We are who we are partly because of historical circumstances that existed during our formative years, or pressures to conform to customary gender standards in mainstream societies. For example, gendered standards of behavior expectations easily trap us into particular patterns of actions when we cannot be sufficiently objective about making commitments. Social intelligence prompts us to reassess how we act in relation to social possibilities, and aiming to be objective safeguards us from resuming problematic individual and social habits that limited our goals and accomplishments in the past.

Gender Responsibilities

Objectivity helps us to define and live our gender responsibilities, at the same time that social intelligence shows us ways to practice gender in everyday life. However, we not only live our genders, but also affect others by how we live our genders. Therefore, we need to resolve to accomplish optimal outcomes for others as well as for ourselves whenever possible in the present for the future.

Social intelligence increases our objectivity, by heightening our awareness of gender and other major social influences, as we gradually assume responsibilities for the well-being of others as well as ourselves. For example, our working knowledge of families, beliefs, social classes, cultures, and societies shows us how to address significant social issues, so that more people benefit from gender freedom than experience the restrictiveness of gender controls. When we are socially intelligent we become more responsible historical actors, who work with others cooperatively and productively to increase the common good and social justice.

We mature through increasing our objectivity and social intelligence, and at the same time undertake more carefully selected responsibilities for the well-being of all. This means that we are more thoughtful about formulating goals that increase the common good in the present for the future. When we use social intelligence to clarify our priorities, we give more time and attention to significant social issues, so that our genders better humankind in the world as well as in individual lives.

VII. Objectivity and Gender

We use our social intelligence and objectivity to understand social influences, so that they do not dominate the directions we take in our everyday decisions and commitments. We avoid this only by continuing to live according to social intelligence principles, because our decisions and commitments are life itself. For example, we increase and maintain our objectivity by examining our gender responsibilities in relation to the five major social influences of families, beliefs, social classes, and societies.

Our families may either support or drain our emotional resources, so that we are more or less effective in accomplishing our preferred gender goals. Consequently, our first concern should be to maintain our objectivity, so that we function more effectively in our families, and family members are freer to express their genders through expansive rather than limited goals. When we create social conditions of freedom and confidence in our families, members of our youngest generations are more likely to make commitments to increase the common good and social justice.

Similarly, social intelligence helps us to address issues about our beliefs more objectively. This helps us to discover the extent to which gender limits our social responsibilities. Because beliefs are motivators for social actions, we assume more meaningful responsibilities by letting go of our limited past beliefs about gender, and by assuming more expansive beliefs about gender for the present and future.

Social intelligence also guides us to be more objective by putting social classes in perspective. For example, we benefit from using social facts to deepen our understanding of social classes, their dominance, and their impacts on our decisions and commitments. Our increased objectivity about these facts suggests that social classes often regulated our genders in socially acceptable ways that ultimately reduced our energies and motivations. Thus, we too easily sacrificed many good intentions about reforming our genders, by conforming to others' gendered standards, rather than pursuing our own goals of gender innovation and change.

Social intelligence encourages us to turn to cultures that refresh and reorient our gendered actions more objectively. Cultures are vital sources of both traditional and modern values about genders. We need to select those values we want to be our own, in order to be more objective and more socially intelligent. For example, we assume responsibilities for the gender well-being of all when we are motivated by more objective, socially intelligent cultural values such as equality, inclusiveness, diversity, cooperation, and openness. Ultimately, acknowledging our gender privileges may motivate us to assist others to gain similar gender freedoms.

The last of the five major social influences on social intelligence, objectivity, and gender responsibilities is societies. This reflects historical changes that impact gender choices and gender similarities or differences. For example, societies show marked contrasts in their acceptance of varied sexualities and sexual orientations, which underlie societal controls of gender. Conditions of war or political tension within and among societies both limit and increase the extent to which people are motivated to change gender responsibilities, such as assuming leadership in resolving public social issues. Consequently, we aim to be sufficiently objective to select more egalitarian gender responsibilities, as we usher in new worlds for the present and future.

Gender Fulfillment

We use social intelligence to increase our objectivity, in order to improve the likelihood that we will be fulfilled through expressing our genders. Objectivity gives us the broadest possible range of choices of genders, sexualities, and sexual orientations, so that we gradually gain more control over our gendered destinies. We are no longer passive pawns of fate, who merely repeat patterns of behavior that have gone before us. Rather, we seize opportunities to increase the common good, in order to be true historical actors.

Objectivity helps us to be our most authentic selves, so that becoming socially intelligent directs us to live up to our existential challenges to live fully, and to make the most of being who we really are. For example, we begin to care less about pleasing others even our most significant others—so that we are freer to pursue our preferred goals of contributing to the common good.

Moreover, when we understand how being objective multiplies our choices of what to decide and what to do, we are more likely to eventually achieve gender fulfillment.

Social intelligence requires us to educate ourselves about our gender options. Consequently, we pay close attention to the complexities and importance of genders, sexualities, and sexual orientations in our families, communities, and societies. We also maintain our objectivity in this learning process, by examining how we relate to our genders in our families, beliefs, social classes, cultures, and societies—the five major social influences that govern our social intelligence.

Families are foundations of our social intelligence, because the emotional sources of our actions and commitments flow from our ongoing experiences of family interdependence and interaction. We tend to maintain our objectivity and broad perspectives in our world views, largely because our relatives originally taught us how to see ourselves, others, and our opportunities. Thus, gender fulfillment is achieved by using family starting points to understand genders, and by moving toward more objective ideals through taking advantage of a wider variety of family choices than was initially apparent.

Our beliefs also need to become more objective and freer by increasing our social intelligence. When we understand and critically assess the usefulness of our beliefs, we are less beholden to their distortions and emphases. Opening our minds, through becoming more socially intelligent, depends on being more objective in our value choices and actions. For example, we deliberately choose beliefs with ideals that aim directly to increase the common good and social justice, so that we are more fulfilled. Beliefs are usually powerful, just because they give us clusters of values that can guide us in many different situations and circumstances.

Due to the fact that social classes often dominate our goals, life styles, and accomplishments, we need to control the extent to which we conform to others' social class expectations. Cultivating objectivity enhances our awareness of the pervasiveness and power of different social class pressures. When we refuse to be directed by social class standards or social mobility imperatives, we gradually succeed in becoming more authentic selves through our varied gender accomplishments. We no longer try to accomplish social class goals, but stay truer to who we are, and increase the well-being of others as well as gain fulfillment.

Cultures are ever-present sources of values and ideals, which replenish us when we falter in achieving our most significant goals. For example, we give our attention to less popular or less widely respected values such as equality, inclusiveness, diversity, cooperation, and openness, as we usher in improved futures for genders. Equality, inclusiveness, diversity, cooperation, and openness are also gender and sexuality values, which motivate us to increase social justice and the common good. Staying focused on these new values allows us to let go of cultural values which are not conducive to achieving gender fulfillment.

Gender fulfillment also results from considering genders in relation to societies, especially when we try to improve gender fulfillment by being more objective about our societies. The social context of our societies yields broad objective views of genders, especially when we compare our societies with other global societies. We become responsible historical actors who fulfill their genders, sexualities, and sexual orientations by continuing to learn about genders in different societies. Social facts about genders, sexualities, and sexual orientations strengthen our social intelligence and objectivity, as well as our gender fulfillment.

VIII. Historical Actors and Gender

Social intelligence gives us new vantage points from which to view and assess our genders, sexualities, sexual orientations, gender choices, gender responsibilities, and gender fulfillment. For example, by making deliberate efforts to be objective, we grasp more fully how easily we are manipulated through our genders, sexualities, and sexual orientations. We also realize the extent to which we may not be sufficiently aware of the significance of our gender choices, gender responsibilities, and gender fulfillment. In these ways, social intelligence introduces us to alternative worlds of panoramic views of gender options, which flow from the social realities of genders, sexualities, and sexual orientations in particular situations.

As we become more aware of our capacities to be socially intelligent, as well as our different ways to increase our social intelligence, we see that attributes such as gender—which we may have previously considered to be purely individual, personal, and genetic—have vitally important social dimensions. For example, our genders are not innate propensities, as much as they are socially conditioned habits of thought and cultural practices. Social intelligence helps us to recognize our genders as significant components of our sexualities, that sometimes have the power to transcend or over-ride biological or physiological individual and social inclinations in our most reactive sexual behaviors.

Our genders are also important integral aspects of our identities. In many respects we choose our genders, and to a certain extent how we express our sexualities, at the same time that we learn to be women or men in complex global societies. Strengthening our social intelligence helps us to appreciate, for example, how patterns in genders, sexualities, and sexual orientations are expressed historically through different time periods, which increases our responsibilities to define current and future trends in terms of genders, sexualities, and sexual orientations.

Therefore, we increase our social intelligence in order to be more aware historical actors with respect to our gender choices. When we are more objective, we usually make more astute choices about how to express our genders in life outcomes and societal well-being. For example, we see the extent to which we may or may not live according to our most cherished gender values, which requires us to make changes in our priorities. Thus, being socially intelligent historical actors enhances our capacities to both understand our genders and use our genders productively.

One of the goals of becoming aware, responsible historical actors is to know and live our genders according to objectives that increase the common good and social justice. Being an historical actor allows us not just to feel and express our genders directly through our sexualities, but also to rectify or balance some of the imbalances and injustices that flow from traditional or customary gender beliefs and practices. When we are historical actors we not only try to take advantage of different gender values and gender outcomes, but also continue to question the extent to which we really accomplish what we set out to do, especially when this depends on our understanding of genders and sexualities. Socially intelligent lives include correcting our behavior, especially when we contradict our own best intentions and purposes.

Cultivating social intelligence and being historical actors do not make us look solely to the past for examples of how to guide and express our genders. Rather, we get as informed as possible about ways in which individuals and populations deal with gender and sexualities through time, so that we make more serious-minded revisions in how to create better futures. For example, we focus on seeing where we are going with respect to our genders and sexualities, so that new social realities will minimize social injustices in gender and sexual practices.

VIII. Historical Actors and Gender

When social intelligence enlightens us about what gender is, and how gender helps us to create better future worlds, we can use it to guide our goals and actions as historical actors. Being historical actors gives us the most meaningful broad views of our gendered lives, and acting in accordance with historical changes inspires our efforts to accomplish meaningful gender goals with like-minded others. We are all historical actors, whether we realize this or not, and we can all benefit from using social intelligence to fulfill our missions as historical actors.

Gender Defined

Social intelligence shows us that historically populations have often polarized their definitions of masculinity and femininity. Consequently, social expectations for men and women based on these definitions have been unreal, imbalanced, and possibly complementary but unjust. For example, the much discussed harmony between contrasting cultural expectations for men and women has often been used to perpetuate power differences between men and women.

One of the most significant problems of polarizing distinctions between men and women is that men and women are frequently more alike than unlike in their values and dreams. In reality, however, social traditions have upheld men's rights rather than women's rights, so that gender role expectations for men and women tend to reinforce historical differences in power or privileges between men and women. Consequently, gender definitions are often distorted by artificially imposed arbitrary gender contrasts, so that social class differences in men's and women's destinies are perpetuated.

Social intelligence helps us to examine our definitions of genders critically within meaningful cultural and societal contexts. For example, historical experiences of genders and sexualities show us how collective behavior patterns in genders and sexualities change through time, regardless of whether individual or shared efforts are made to bring about particular gender goals. Although societies and individuals need to adapt to either changing or static gender definitions, gender identities inevitably bring about new shifts in gender behavior when they are deliberately constructed or reconstructed.

On a personal level, we understand the five major social influences of families, beliefs, social classes, cultures, and societies better when we scrutinize whole ranges of definitions of genders and sexualities used in our own families, beliefs, social classes, cultures, and societies. Consequently, we become more effective historical actors when we are aware of the assumptions we make about our genders and sexualities, as well as the expectations that significant others have in our families, beliefs, social classes, cultures, and societies.

When we want to change specific ways in which we live as historical actors, we must make our definitions of gender explicit, as well as our understanding of what our gender definitions mean for accomplishing varied goals as historical actors. When we increase the clarity of our starting points of gender definitions, it is easier to focus on our gender intentions, successes, and failures. This also enhances our awareness of what we should do as historical actors.

Defining genders is a foundation for formulating and understanding our gender identities. Gender definitions show us the many ways in which we absorb female or male values to become real women or real men. Because the degree of authenticity of our gender identities makes our whole beings come alive or die, we are beholden to what our gender identities and gender definitions are. They also motivate us to accomplish our gendered goals in particular ways.

When we are historical actors we may decide that our gender identities should over-ride all our other value choices and concerns. Or, we may consider that our gender identities are merely incidental to more objective goals that we prefer to pursue, such as improving education for members of low income social classes. Whether or not we give salience to our gender identities and gender definitions, the content and intensity of our gender definitions determine much of our behavior. Whatever we do, our gender definitions are basic sources that generate energies, as well as motives to increase the common good or social justice. Furthermore, social intelligence makes us more aware of what our current gender definitions are, and how we might change gender definitions that do not help us to produce our preferred end results.

Many of our gender definitions name subtle aspects of our sexualities and sexual orientations, so that our attitudes about our bodies are strongly influenced by our overall views of ourselves. This does not make the embodiment of our gender definitions unimportant, but rather shows us that much of the power to control or override our genetic, biological, or physiological drives flows from our understanding of social contexts. Even though socially intelligent perspectives may not consistently be all-important ways to view the world, they help to set the scene for developing our social awareness as historical actors, and for making changes in our gender definitions that have significant historical consequences.

Gender and Sexuality

Some sexual characteristics of human beings do not appear to change through history or evolution, but there is no doubt that the sexual practices of human beings often vary considerably depending on families, beliefs, social classes, cultures, and history. To the extent that our genders are physiological or biological, we may also discover common denominators among the rich arrays of sexual practices employed, if only around acts of procreation. For example, when we are socially intelligent about our gender choices, we understand that in order to perpetuate populations we must have replacement levels of births, which presuppose specific heterosexual acts or gender practices.

Our genders are not totally governed by our biological sexes, but physiological aspects of our being are vital to our survival as individuals and populations, as well as socially significant in their own right. Therefore, sexuality is a social resource that must be managed wisely if we are to survive. At the same time, historical variations in sexual practices have important implications and consequences for particular qualities of life, such as the freedom to express ourselves sexually. Thus, historical eras may be usefully characterized as being more or less permissive in their regulation of human sexualities. Historical trends suggest that civilization itself may ultimately depend on sexual practices and their refinements.

When we are socially intelligent, we often accept the task of increasing our social intelligence as a lifetime endeavor and commitment. This means that we recognize that the social influences of genders are affected by continuities in our beliefs about sexualities, as well as by the relatively unchanging aspects of our biological sexualities. For example, we may conduct ourselves as women and men more according to our beliefs in sexualities, rather than in direct relation to the biological facts of our sexualities. In these respects, our physiology as men and women is inevitably affected by—and to some extent controlled by—our cultural beliefs about sexualities.

Nevertheless, socially intelligent historical actors realize that our cultural beliefs about the constant sexual characteristics in human populations are subject to change. Although we have tended to dissociate biological sexual imperatives from our awareness of the social characteristics of genders through time, we cannot afford to separate these two aspects of reality from each other. If we are objective about the influences of biological sex in our behavior, we need to understand that biological sex interacts with social imperatives, which makes us behave in different kinds of acceptable or unacceptable ways.

Historical actors control their decision-making in relation to the goals they aim for in conducting their everyday lives. For example, historical actors acknowledge that human beings are beholden to responsibilities to reproduce their populations, as well as responsibilities to construct better futures for all. Therefore, sexualities are vital aspects of genders, gender practices, and gender expressions. However, history has shown us that gender, sexuality, and sexual orientation are not fate for increasing numbers of people. Our biological characteristics need not determine our life outcomes and ideals.

Social facts about the interconnectedness of sexualities and genders suggest that we cannot understand genders fully unless we acknowledge the pervasiveness and power of sexualities in the total scheme of life. One of the most significant choices we have, in recognizing sexualities' links to genders, is that sexuality need not dominate our lives. Consequently, other aspects of our everyday behavior are not necessarily overshadowed by our procreative needs or our needs for sexual expression. We can opt to lead lives that improve the qualities of life in societies, rather than act solely to express our sexualities.

Consequently, being an historical actor requires thoughtful assessments of our options and commitments, so that we participate fully in freeing ourselves and other people from at least the potential dominance of our sexualities. We accomplish this by maintaining productive gender protocols, and by understanding and acting upon other complex characteristics of our social lives. For example, we live more fully when we transcend some of the restrictive or destructive aspects of the biological imperatives of our sexualities, and promote more just social conditions for populations and civilizations. Historical actors commit themselves to undertake gender and sexuality missions, for example, so that they move societies forward in their existential quests to meet the needs of all in meaningful ways.

Gender and Sexual Orientation

Gender is related to sexual orientations as well as sexualities. Although our sexual predispositions may well be largely innate rather than learned, we can decide how to disclose or hide our sexual orientations in our complex cultures. The fact that we control how we present our sexual orientations to others means that we have choices in what we make of our genders and sexual orientations. Social intelligence therefore guides our gendered actions, so that we express our sexual orientations responsibly, as well as work to achieve social justice for all.

Particular sexual orientations have been more acceptable in some societies than others, frequently depending on their historical and social circumstances. For example, even though some societies accepted people's homosexual orientations from time to time, heterosexual societies have tended to be dominant in both ancient and modern eras. This does not necessarily mean that heterosexuality is a fixed component of human nature, but rather that heterosexuality has been used as a way to procreate and raise children in most societies to the present. However, recent decades have seen many deeper questions raised about alternatives to heterosexuality in both traditional and modern societies.

Even though human beings seem to have some flexibility in expressing their sexualities, sexual orientations often appear to be difficult or impossible to change. Furthermore, even though some individuals and populations have relatively narrow views about which sexual orientations are preferable, or considered to be morally superior, people inevitably benefit from embracing differences in sexual orientations in their societies, so that social justice can exist for all. Prejudice and discrimination against some sexual orientations do not serve populations well, and are counter-productive in efforts to create better societies.

Because sexual orientations produce their own cultures in families, beliefs, social classes, and societies, we need social intelligence to understand and accept our genders and their connections to sexual orientations. When we see how families, beliefs, social classes, cultures, and societies reflect patterns of popularity, prejudice, discrimination, and tolerance for sexual orientations, we understand crucial dimensions of our genders and sexualities. We are who we are because of the social influences of our families, beliefs, social classes, cultures, and societies, as well as because of our genders, sexualities, and sexual orientations.

Social intelligence guides our behavior, so that we do not engage in destructive gender, sexuality, and sexual orientation practices. Also, as we become more aware historical actors, we may decide to participate in ways and means to change societies' problematic attitudes about genders, sexualities, and sexual orientations, because of our commitments to increase the common good and social justice. For example, as long as particular individuals suffer from prejudice and discrimination, due to their sexual orientations, whole populations cannot function well. Therefore, we need to continue educating ourselves, so that we become more socially intelligent and work together effectively to reduce negative, destructive attitudes about sexual orientations.

Historical actors commit themselves to improve social conditions, in order to accept sexual orientations more fully. They also persist in learning about social issues in sexual orientations through time in families, beliefs, social classes, cultures, and societies. When we recognize the pervasiveness of the negative effects of prejudices and discrimination in social practices related to different sexual orientations, we are more able to be objective about our individual and collective ignorance or cruelty in maintaining these behaviors. At the same time that we aim to create better societies for the future, we must change problematic patterns of emotional dependencies in our populations. Furthermore, we must realize that prejudice and discrimination about sexual orientations will prevent us from establishing socially intelligent values of equality, inclusiveness, diversity, cooperation, and openness in our current and future societies.

Clarifying our attitudes about sexual orientations is therefore an essential stage of recognizing our choices about genders, gender responsibilities, and gender fulfillment. However, unless we make direct efforts to reduce barriers to achieving social justice for people with all sexual orientations, our socially intelligent actions will be limited and unable to pursue or attain our preferred goals. We must make commitments to do whatever we can to rectify imbalances in public knowledge and attitudes about varied sexual orientations, so that we are more united in choosing constructive and effective social strategies to reinforce the well-being of all in our societies.

Gender Choices

When we become historical actors, we make more deliberate gender choices. With our deepened understanding of the power, complexities, and pervasiveness of the five major social influences of families, beliefs, social classes, cultures, and societies, we see

127

that people live gendered lives in all societies. Because no sphere of human activity is devoid of gender concerns, we benefit from being aware of how our genders, sexualities, and sexual orientations affect who we are and what we do. This means that we not only need to scrutinize what is actually going on in our lives, but also how we make choices about our genders in all situations. Our heightened socially intelligent awareness shows us more clearly what the implications or consequences of our old and new views of gender social realities are, for example, as well as what options we have about genders and sexual orientations.

We do not need to be constantly preoccupied by assessing the significance and complexity of our gender choices. However, we gain from building habits of thinking that include broad social intelligence perspectives, especially from the points of view of families, beliefs, social classes, cultures, and societies. When we increase our social intelligence, for example, we try to account for both the world of personal intimacy and the world of globalization from these viewpoints. Our socially intelligent breadth of concern opens up new vistas of how societies could be, and what we want to accomplish during our lifetimes.

Increasing our social intelligence sooner or later includes becoming more aware historical actors. For example, we learn how to inform our thinking and actions with social facts and social realities related to families, beliefs, social classes, cultures, and societies. These five major social influences reflect emotional undertows of pressures to conform and go with the flow of others' priorities, even when they may not be in the best interests of us or our societies. When we aim to become freer in relation to our genders, it behooves us to understand the extent to which we negotiate or give up our precious autonomy and uniqueness in relation to others, because this causes us to lose effectiveness in our own lives and societies.

Persisting in making efforts to live according to social intelligence principles, when we are aware and responsible historical actors, is a sacred quest in that these struggles predictably increase our personal and social freedom to some extent. Human beings are existentially concerned about living fully, and we are responsible for the choices we make along these lines. For example, when we succeed in making gender choices that express our highest values, we simultaneously increase our personal and social fulfillment.

Historical actors not only see their gender choices as being influenced by local situations, but also as being subjected to national and international historical trends. Even though we may not be aware of the impacts of past histories on what we do in the present, these influences exist and often prevail, unless we take charge of our situations through making more deliberate gender choices. We do not necessarily aim to become more masculine or more feminine in our responses to social conditions, but rather free ourselves sufficiently from gender pressures, so that we live as though gender expectations are not determining powers.

Denying the influence of conventional gender expectations in our own social situations may not reduce stresses from existing gender pressures in the short run, but making this choice helps us to clarify our decisions, so that we more nearly approach our preferred goals. Social intelligence is merely a tool that enhances our awareness of how to increase the common good and social justice. When we are historical actors, we understand our given circumstances more thoroughly, as well as make wiser decisions, in light of the power and complexities of those strong social influences that might otherwise engulf us in our efforts to create improved societies.

Wise gender choices, from the points of view of history and ongoing broad social perspectives, are significant achievements in their own right. In fact, gender choices have the power to transform our experiences and our worlds. For example, we can change the foundations of our being through our gender choices, because we create significant personal and social changes at the same time that we try to respond constructively to historical pressures. Making wise gender choices is a significant goal of being socially intelligent, which enables us to move more directly toward accomplishing improvements in social justice.

Gender Responsibilities

Being an historical actor increases our gender responsibilities and, at the same time that we meet our gender responsibilities, we become more effective historical actors. Learning and using social intelligence is not an easy ride. We heighten our awareness about social influences in and among societies when we recognize what social intelligence is, with the result that many questions about responsibilities inevitably emerge. For example, who is responsible for the gender qualities of my life? Who is responsible for the gender qualities of the lives of those who suffer in our societies and throughout the world? What can I do to improve gender social conditions for all in societies? What do we need to do to teach the next generations about maintaining gender values which help individuals and societies to survive and fulfill the needs of their populations? How do responsibilities for genders, sexualities, and sexual orientations differ?

Being an historical actor, which is a relatively advanced stage of being socially intelligent, raises these issues because we consider major social influences—families, beliefs, social classes, cultures, and societies—when we make decisions and formulate our preferred goals as historical actors. For example, when we acknowledge our historical connections to our genders, we shed light on what our responsibilities are as knowing or educated individuals. We are socially intelligent when we make commitments to learn about social influences and their impacts on past and present historical conditions for the future. In fact, unless we deliberately maintain broad perspectives about families, beliefs, social classes, cultures, and societies, we will be ineffectual historical actors who regress to earlier ways of thinking from being entrapped by these social influences.

Considering gender responsibilities, from the perspective of being an historical actor, draws attention to the social fact that our historical efforts to increase the common good or strengthen social justice need to be accomplished by working with others. For example, unless we know how to locate and cooperate with likeminded others to accomplish our socially intelligent goals, we will not be able to attain our objectives. Working alone is by no means as effective as cooperating with people who share similar historical perspectives, especially views which focus on the five major social influences of families, beliefs, social classes, cultures, and societies. By contrast individual efforts are too easily associated with competitive self interests, which are not universal in scope.

In some respects, historical tasks require us to balance staying objective about the social conditions we aim to improve, with how to implement the most effective goals to reach these ends. There is nothing trite or easy about this venture. We must base our actions on the social facts of particular situations, so that we work effectively to develop reliable strategies with those who have also made commitments to increase the common good and social justice for genders, sexualities, and sexual orientations. Furthermore, unless we continue to account for the power and complexities of the five major social influences of families, beliefs, social classes, and societies, we will not be able to coordinate our responsible actions effectively.

We continue to learn what our responsibilities are as historical actors. We are not born with these sensibilities, but rather become knowledgeable about how social our lives are, as well as how useful social intelligence can be, in order to sort out some of the complexities in social influences which otherwise lead to our suffering or demise. Furthermore, we must maintain our social intelligence if we are to be responsible historical actors, because much depends on continuing to be well-informed in increasing the common good and social justice.

Making sure that we are responsible about our genders is a precondition of gender fulfillment. This is an important reason why we need to focus on significant questions such as what it takes to be responsible in our gendered actions at individual, communal, societal, and global levels of thinking and concern, especially because we need to cooperate with others in order to harness our resources and meet our goals. The sum total of what we do in relation to families, beliefs, social classes, cultures, and societies, influences the most significant qualities of our lives, as well as teaches us about others' social conditions and social realities.

Gender Fulfillment

We strive to be socially intelligent about our genders in part because this helps us to attain more satisfying levels of gender fulfillment. Social intelligence calls us to develop our potentials in order to attain greater fulfillment for ourselves and others. Social intelligence also shows us that in order to be whole, we must find ways to express our genders, sexualities, and sexual orientations, as well as our best intentions toward ourselves, others, our communities, and the world.

In addition to responding to existential imperatives to live fully and well, we develop our potentials so that we are as effective as possible in bringing better worlds into being. Social intelligence helps us to reach goals that bring about these changes, for example, so that we can envision new societies and different ways of being. We heighten our awareness about genders through our social intelligence, and discover how to work with others to increase the common good and social justice.

When we are historical actors we understand that the quality of our lives depends on our connections to the social issues around us. We assess our social situations, as well as the parts we play in perpetuating oppressive social conditions for ourselves and others. We also often research the extent to which we are pressured to conform to social trends that we would rather change than perpetuate.

Thus, social intelligence heightens our awareness of individual and social contradictions. For example, social intelligence guides us to make new value choices, so that we reduce the ways in which we feel emotionally compelled to reinforce conventional values. Consequently, we clarify what we really want to change: social intelligence shows us how to deliberately invest our emotions in constructive values that strengthen rather than destroy civilizations.

We gain fulfillment, including gender fulfillment, when we live by moving in directions that bring us closer to understanding improved new worlds. For example, social intelligence connects us to historical trends, and shows us that we have some control over historical outcomes. Being an historical actor is therefore a significant goal and daily objective, which motivates us to harness our energies in constructive projects with others, in order to increase freedom and fulfillment for all in the long run.

Social intelligence shows us that we cannot be content or complacent about aiming merely to achieve our own gender fulfillment. In the long run we must be concerned about those who are less fortunate than us, who routinely struggle to survive without experiencing real fulfillment or satisfaction. We are fortunate when we can play significant roles in how things are run in our societies, and in deciding what social outcomes could be in more just futures.

Overall, one of our most significant choices is to be fulfilled through our genders. It is all too easy to take things for granted about our genders, to follow the dictates of conventional cultural roles for genders, to live in restricted ways according to narrow definitions of gender, or to ignore calls to be responsible for our own fates and the well-being of others. Passivity kills us when we become victims of others' preferences, others' self interests, and others' lacks of vision for the future. By contrast, a calling to be an historical actor energizes our social intelligence, and realizes our potentials to make better worlds possible for more people each day.

Gender fulfillment flows from going in these constructive directions. We know that we cannot accomplish all our idealistic goals, but we also realize that we need to face in enlightened directions as we go about our daily lives, especially when we commit ourselves to being historical actors. Consequently, we find that we bring satisfaction to us and other people as we work for honorable goals that increase our choices for better lives for all.

Although we may not be able to rest contentedly when we set out initially, as historical actors, to achieve our serious agendas, at least we live more meaningfully with purpose, verve, and direction. Social intelligence teaches us to treasure our genders, sexualities, and sexual orientations as valuable resources that enhance the beauty and vitality of life. This motivates us to cooperate effectively with others, so that we persevere in creating and maintaining societies that nurture equality, inclusiveness, diversity, cooperation, and openness.

IX. Social Justice and Gender

Social intelligence helps us to understand gender more fully, as well as guides us to work for social justice. However, social justice may not be a goal that interests many people. Furthermore, social justice is often such an abstract objective that it seems impossible to assess or attain. Although the vagueness of social justice may not motivate us sufficiently to immediately try to change ourselves or our societies, when social intelligence is applied to social justice goals, it gives us sufficient freedom of choice to solve complex social problems creatively and constructively.

Genders, sexualities, and sexual orientations are significant determining influences in our lives, especially when we lose control of managing ourselves and others in our everyday exchanges. Because of the intrinsic physiological qualities of sexualities and sexual orientations, our genders often seem to be more than the sum total of the social influences that make us who we are. However, many of the social influences that impact us yield meaningful ways to control our genders, sexualities, and sexual orientations, so that we are able to negotiate more deliberately with others.

It is easy to delineate significant social aspects of our genders, sexualities, and sexual orientations. These include strong pressures to conform to others' standards of gender, sexuality, and sexual orientation. For example, we can trace past and present social facts that reveal social realities of societies' prejudices and discrimination about genders, sexualities, and sexual orientation through long periods of time. Because social dimensions of genders, sexualities, and sexual orientations are human-made and not physiologically determined, social intelligence shows us that we can decide to change and adapt differently to social influences around genders, sexualities, and sexual orientations.

Social justice is one of the most significant goals we can work toward each day in expressing our genders, sexualities, and sexual orientations. Although we do not need to focus on social justice at all times, largely because we must deal wholeheartedly with demanding ongoing social issues and social pressures, we can choose the ideal of social justice as a meaningful direction for our daily work, or as enlightenment in how to create and establish more viable social realities. Social intelligence helps us to make significant connections between our social situations and social justice principles, as well as between our genders, sexualities, sexual orientations, and societies based on equality, inclusiveness, diversity, cooperation, and openness.

For example, we can consider equality in terms of specific gender definitions, gender choices, gender responsibilities, and gender fulfillment. In the same way, we can use inclusiveness, diversity, cooperation, and openness to understand others and act according to our socially intelligent gender definitions, gender choices, gender responsibilities, and gender fulfillment. Thus, social justice inspiration, thought, and action invigorate our everyday goals and motives. Consequently, we behave differently each day when social justice is a commitment, purpose, and direction in our lives.

Social intelligence educates us about how contrasting types of social organization—local, national, and global—affect each other, and how societies interact. When we are socially intelligent we choose to learn more about the complexities of past and present social trends in social justice, in order to raise significant questions about current social facts and social realities. In the midst of our research on how to survive more effectively in the social pressures that affect us the most, we see that reducing the power that major social influences have over us improves social justice in our lives and the lives of others.

IX. Social Justice and Gender

We come to recognize that interacting differently in our families, beliefs, social classes, cultures, and societies creates new directions for us and others, and that this enables us to participate more effectively in increasing social justice. We also discover that learning and education are vital tools for accomplishing constructive social changes, because social intelligence shows us how to make connections between social facts, social realities, social possibilities, genders, and social justice.

Social intelligence draws attention to our social dependencies and entrapments, and at the same time suggests that pursuing social justice opens up new worlds for all. For example, when we plan our lives along lines of increasing social justice, or spreading social justice in the world, social intelligence guides us to design reliable and effective strategies based on social facts. Consequently, we are more likely to cooperate with others when social intelligence informs and directs our decision-making and commitments. Thus, to the extent that we express our genders in socially intelligent ways, we also increase social justice in the long run.

Gender Defined

Social justice illumines our socially intelligent definitions of gender and gender identities. This is so because whenever we think of ourselves in the very broad social contexts of social justice, we see ourselves differently. For example, social intelligence helps us to consider who we are in relation to secular globalization structures and processes, while social justice requires us to see who we are in relation to ethical or moral contexts, such as the common good.

Whereas most people may not consider seriously how they interact with the world at large as well as with specific local situations, they are sometimes willing to identify ways in which their genders are influenced by others' gender behavior in communities, societies, and globalization. Social intelligence prompts us to raise questions about our families, beliefs, social classes, cultures, and societies as well as our genders, so that we gradually learn how to assess the impacts of these major social influences on our understanding of genders, and on actually living out our genders, sexualities, and sexual orientations.

Everyday observations of how people interact in their communities show us that gender expectations are frequently oppressive and coercive, as well as difficult to change. For example, parents routinely use gender standards to restrict or control the behavior of their sons and daughters. However, whenever this happens, the children inevitably feel trapped by how their parents think they should behave as boys or girls. Consequently, when these children mature, they yearn for the freedom to choose how to define their personal and gender identities. Social intelligence encourages us to define our own genders now, so that we modify the impacts of some of the most significant complex and powerful social influences in our lives.

Social justice enlightens what may appear to be private, personal struggles, because it is important for us to understand how we exist in relation to the world at large, or at least in the context of our own societies. For example, when we recognize inequalities and imbalances in both local and national arenas— especially in relation to genders—we are moved, at best, to make decisions and act, so that these social injustices are rectified. Social intelligence encourages us to use our knowledge of social facts to create better worlds responsibly. Moreover, when we are socially intelligent, we know that unless our worlds are more equal, inclusive, diverse, cooperative, and open, we will ultimately destroy our civilizations.

In these respects, social intelligence considers that changing our views of ourselves, our communities, our societies, and the world is a crucial precondition of making constructive social changes to increase the common good and social justice. We need to realize that we are integral parts of efforts already being made to design and create better futures, in order to lead more meaningful and purposeful lives. Given this social momentum, our genders are significant energies that we can use to live more thoughtfully. For example, we can choose to define our genders in sufficiently broad social terms to help us to achieve social justice, so that we live more freely with strong genders, sexualities, and sexual orientations.

One of the most important reasons why we should try to define our genders in terms of social justice, is that we can only strengthen and develop our gender identities when we know what we face. Because our identities govern how we act, especially in relation to other people and the goals we want to accomplish, we benefit from assessing which of our gendered responses to life are most worthy of our attention and cultivation. For example, as women we may need to concentrate on being active rather than passive, in order to be sufficiently free to commit ourselves to work on lifetime projects. By contrast, as men, we may need to express our emotions more fully, especially when we get directly involved in improving social conditions to meet human needs.

Strengthening our gender identities encourages us to assess how our sexualities and sexual orientations contribute to our genders and other aspects of our everyday lives. Although the social dimensions of our gender identities may be more apparent than the social dimensions of our sexualities and sexual orientations, how we understand our sexualities and sexual orientations helps us to see important social justice issues in different situations. Furthermore, it is often only when we know how our lives are affected by interpersonal and broad social tensions that we can proceed to make viable social justice changes for the present and future.

Gender and Sexuality

Appreciating overlaps between our genders and sexualities is a significant way to understand our genders more fully. However, it is not always clear how our firmer grasp of the importance of genders and sexualities influences our understanding and uses of social justice in our everyday lives. Although we may have already chosen social justice as a strong motivating force in our decision-making, applying our interests and the emotional drives of genders and sexualities to achieving social justice goals is not yet an easy or widespread habit of thought or social practice.

To a certain extent, religious beliefs connect genders and sexualities as relevant aspects of our moral welfare and moral behavior. Unfortunately, these associations are also linked frequently to reinforcing conformity to traditional models of genders and sexualities, such as fairly rigid support for the social ideals of institutional marriage and procreation. Even though these real and true aspects of how individuals and populations past or present have adapted or controlled the sexual behavior of masses of people, patterns in beliefs and morals may not consistently serve the common good and social justice, especially given the vast diversity of behavior and values associated with genders and sexualities.

Social intelligence makes us aware of varied genders and sexualities, as well as their relationships to social justice concerns. For example, both modern education and secular research show that sexual orientations may be largely genetic and therefore not deliberately chosen. Because of this social fact, we are existentially obligated to broaden and deepen our understanding of genders and sexualities. Consequently, from the points of view of social justice, we are increasingly aware that we need to embrace differences in genders and sexualities, if we are to create better worlds today for tomorrow.

Thus, social justice perspectives take us beyond merely comparing and contrasting women's and men's rights. Social intelligence requires us to consider gender and social concerns about all sexualities and sexual orientations in order to meet the real needs of populations, whatever their ages or social classes. By contrast, social justice shows us that we must not only deliberately cultivate a deep appreciation of individual gender and sexual differences, but also educate ourselves in ways of thinking that go beyond the restrictive gender and sexual categories of traditional or conventional understanding and actions about gender.

In these respects, social justice ideals open up our overly narrow attitudes or bigotry about genders and sexualities. We are not necessarily socially intelligent when we merely accept mainstream thinking about sensitive gender and sexual matters.

Rather, social intelligence requires us to look squarely at, and assess, all gender and sexuality social facts in our everyday lives and moral ideals. For example, social intelligence teaches us how to discern distinctions between different genders and sexualities, so that we do not unnecessarily restrict the individual and social lives of members of our present and future populations.

Both social intelligence and social justice urge us to more fully embrace the many socially significant nuances of genders and sexualities. First, we make sure that we are living according to socially intelligent principles ourselves. Next, we strive to develop historical awareness and enlightened social concerns about social justice. These broad perspectives inform and direct our socially intelligent behavior. They also prevent us from abusing social intelligence, so that we do not manipulate others to meet our own self-interests.

When we live according to social intelligence principles we decide how we contribute to the common good, which allows social justice to guide us to address broad spheres of gender concerns. Social justice is a necessary goal, because in many respects our genders and sexualities are often too easily harnessed to support societies' status quo through the guise of increasing the common good. This does not mean that the common good is an unworthy goal, but rather that people sometimes understand the common good in more restricted ways than the ideal of social justice implies.

Ultimately, social justice enables us to think outside the box of conventional views, so that we imagine better futures more clearly, and at the same time relate directly to the needs of whole populations in modern globalization. For example, social justice enables us to address the broadest implications of genders and sexualities effectively, so that we stay relevant in articulating gender and sexuality goals that need to be addressed now for the future. Furthermore, we use social intelligence and social justice to assess and change the complex nuances of genders and sexualities in our families, beliefs, social classes, cultures, and societies.

Gender and Sexual Orientation

Sexual orientation, like gender, is often used as a base for social classes in modern societies. For example, heterosexuality tends to be given a higher social class status than homosexuality, largely because heterosexuality is usually a majority rather than a minority sexual orientation. However, social facts in these trends show that members of populations who have heterosexual orientations often feel threatened by minority homosexual claims to equality, with the result that strong tensions persist between these two social classes.

Other social classes in modern societies are also related to different sexual orientations. For example, bisexual and transgender groups frequently have lower social class statuses than heterosexual or homosexual people. Because these social class trends persist in modern societies, we must consider sexual orientation as a significant emotional issue which divides populations, and shows the continued existence of sexual orientation taboos in modern societies—even though sexual orientation prohibitions are no longer as clear-cut or as destructive now as they were previously.

Social intelligence gives us new ways to understand and nullify some of our destructive reactions to sexual orientations, especially from social justice perspectives. For example, when we increase our social intelligence we deliberately define genders, sexualities, and sexual orientations in ways that neutralize pernicious social class differences and taboos among people with varied sexual orientations. When we use social intelligence to identify and emphasize social aspects of sexual orientations, our socially intelligent awareness may guide us to be bolder in changing our given gender situations. For example, instead of being content to run away and hide from societies because we support homosexual rights and lifestyles, social intelligence helps us to take bold stands to uphold our beliefs in equality with regard to gender and sexual fulfillment in societies. Applying social intelligence and social justice principles enables us to participate more directly in creating social conditions that make this happen for ourselves and others.

142

IX. Social Justice and Gender

Social intelligence teaches us that whatever we learn can be changed. This socially intelligent principle suggests that we can modify our attitudes and beliefs about our given sexual orientations rather than our sexual orientations per se. For example, we adopt social justice as a source of moral ideals to direct our everyday lives, so that we make the best use of our talents to accomplish shared goals about sexual orientations and genders. We also educate publics about the importance of deliberately selecting social justice values—such as equality, inclusiveness, diversity, cooperation, and openness—to guide our decision-making and commitments, so that we improve social conditions for genders and sexual orientations in the present for the future.

In many respects, because of the persistence of social taboos against minority sexual orientations, it is difficult for individuals, communities, societies, and global groups to accept and integrate individual and social issues about diverse sexual orientations in their everyday exchanges. This is partly due to the vulnerability of sexual orientation minorities in both local and global communities.

Consequently, our existential choice in this social dilemma is either to move in directions which prepare us for more equal, productive societies, or to prolong entrenched gender and sexual orientation social injustices in the current status quo. Because social intelligence clearly urges us to act by responding to future needs as well as contemporary social pressures, we benefit from applying this principle to our decision-making and commitments. This helps us to ensure that whatever we do brings about more freedom for all sexual orientations in the present and future.

Only when we see our genders, sexualities, and sexual orientations through the broad perspectives of social intelligence and social justice can we take sufficient enlightened action for our shared well-being in the present and future. We have to muster moral fortitude to face and deal with the social facts of sexual orientation injustices, rather than accommodate to the entrenched social injustices in genders, sexualities, and sexual orientations.

Moreover, the tenacity of unfair gender and sexual taboos can only be loosened effectively through designing and taking socially intelligent social justice actions.

We choose to increase our social intelligence, and to let social intelligence guide our sexual orientation actions, which involves situations where it is difficult to apply social justice values. Social intelligence keeps us on track in our research on social facts about gender and sexual orientations, so that we maintain our commitments to make the world a more just place for ourselves and others. We also bring the spirit of social justice to bear on easing the stranglehold that the five major social influences of families, beliefs, social classes, cultures, and societies have on who we are and what we do as gendered, sexually oriented individuals and groups.

Gender Choices

Defining our genders, sexualities, and sexual orientations according to social intelligence and social justice principles increases our gender options. When we deliberately seek to increase our social intelligence and work toward social justice, we think outside conventional views, and maintain broad frames of reference that allow us to envision improved but realistic futures. At the same time that we consider our social conditions in these ways, we see choices that we were not aware of before.

In order to become fully conscious socially intelligent beings, we acknowledge the power and complexities of the five major social influences of families, beliefs, social classes, cultures, and societies. By doing this we loosen the overly tight ties that many of us have to these significant spheres of social interaction. Increasing our objectivity about being connected to families, beliefs, social classes, cultures, and societies frees us to be more authentic in our personal and gender choices, so that we make meaningful commitments to contribute to the common good and social justice. For example, we continue to see connections between populations and families, beliefs, social classes, cultures, and societies as well as between individuals and families, beliefs, social classes, cultures, and societies.

IX. Social Justice and Gender

Our socially intelligent awareness prepares us to apply these broad perspectives to all aspects of our daily lives. No part of what we deal with each day—whatever our social circumstances are—is untouched by these five major social influences, so we have plenty to concern ourselves with as we make decisions and act. We become more aware of the purposes and directions of our lives, in order to change what we are doing when our beliefs or actions contradict what we want to accomplish.

Thus, social justice brings coherence to our decision-making. For example, when we consider values which reflect social justice ideals—such as equality, inclusiveness, diversity, cooperation, and openness—we appreciate the social fact that we choose our assumptions as well as our actions. What do we really believe about social realities and our own situations? What are the social facts of our genders, sexualities, and sexual orientations? To what extent do our genders, sexualities, and sexual orientations predispose us to increase the common good and social justice?

In these respects, social intelligence is a tool which connects us meaningfully to social justice goals. For example, when we understand the social influences in our lives more fully, we make wiser choices about our commitments, and are more discerning about working with others to accomplish social justice goals. Identifying our genders, sexualities, and sexual orientations increases our breadth of vision, so that we use our resources of genders, sexualities, and sexual orientations more productively and effectively.

Although we can surmise that women, men, boys, and girls may see themselves as having different choices due to their genders, sexualities, and sexual orientations, we are surprisingly more alike than unlike with respect to our preferred options. For example, because human beings want fulfillment, they search out how to make contributions that count in the total scheme of things. Being socially intelligent suggests different routes to accomplish similar goals, especially through the prism of social justice. We become advocates for our own needs, as well as for those who cannot articulate their needs.

Our gender, sexuality, and sexual orientation choices set us on meaningful paths that open up our everyday lives, however stringent our social situations are. Furthermore, we use social intelligence to distinguish between imagined social limits and real restrictions, so that we express ourselves more freely. Although social intelligence does not require us to revolutionize our situations, seemingly slight changes in our choices sometimes transform our lives.

Because social intelligence derives from social facts in families, beliefs, social classes, cultures, and societies, we must continue to review and renew our understanding of our genders, sexualities, and sexual orientations. These important postures to life can be inspired by social justice, so that we may more deliberately focus on changing societies' ways of dealing with genders, sexualities, and sexual orientations, or on changing other problematic concerns like social classes.

In the long run, we need to persist in clarifying what our genders suggest among the complex and powerful social influences that affect us the most. How can we protect ourselves from being victimized by major social influences? How can we make value choices that open up new worlds for today and tomorrow? How can we be true to our genders, sexualities, and sexual orientations, and at the same time meet social justice goals?

Gender Responsibilities

We are more responsible when we deliberately choose what we do, rather than act in response to others' social pressures or expectations. One of the insidious characteristics of genders is that the overly simplistic dualism of male and female is so much taken for granted that we do not realize, or question, this social reality. Rather, we tend to go along with assumptions made about males or females in more or less automatic ways, which predictably limit our freedom of choice and responsibility. It is only when we pay attention to the facts of our social conditioning and their consequences, that we become fully free and responsible in our hopes and actions.

IX. Social Justice and Gender

In these respects, we need to take charge of defining our genders, sexualities, and sexual orientations more clearly, if we are to work with real and effective gender choices and gender responsibilities. We can achieve these results at many levels of social organization—for example, through our families, beliefs, social classes, cultures, and societies—which we now understand through our social intelligence. We develop perspectives on social justice through increasing our social intelligence, which enables us to be more authentic and more effective historical actors, as well as more fulfilled.

Thus, social intelligence opens the door for us to assume more chosen responsibilities, while at the same time social justice helps us to connect what we want to accomplish with ongoing currents of historical change. For example, social justice inspires us to develop more comprehensive vocations to contribute to the common good. When we see our experiences of genders, sexualities, and sexual orientations in relation to equality, inclusiveness, diversity, cooperation, and openness, we more easily discover and take on missions to be more responsible in conducting our everyday lives. This increases our senses of meaning, purpose, and direction, as well as makes us more effective in achieving our objectives.

At times we may find it easier to give up on formulating goals to achieve lofty vocations before we can identify them sufficiently clearly for ourselves. However, when we choose to live without defining any purposes or directions, we reduce our fulfillment so much, that even our defeatist postures are difficult to sustain. At best, this lack of satisfaction may eventually reinforce our commitments to try to increase the common good and social justice. Our personal and social dissatisfactions can gradually motivate us to harness our gender and sexual energies to accomplish responsible social justice goals.

We make considerable progress in these areas when we continue to go back to interacting differently in the five major social spheres of families, beliefs, social classes, cultures, and societies. We do this because these influences largely determine our social intelligence and whoever we decide we are. For example, we may aim to assume responsibilities for making sure that all members of our families are cared for by working with others to meet their real needs. Furthermore, in order to be effective in accomplishing responsible social justice goals in our families, we must continue to scrutinize our beliefs. This ensures that our social justice priorities stay sufficiently clear to guide our responsible actions to meet social justice goals.

Deliberately interacting with the five major social influences differently also requires us to continue to review our social class exchanges. This is especially pertinent because gender, sexuality, and sexual orientation are viewed as social classes in both traditional and modern societies. When we assess how we interact with social classes, we see more clearly how our actions increase rather than reduce social inequalities in our assumptions, attitudes, and results. Only when we are committed to reducing social class extremes and contrasts in resources and opportunities are we truly responsible for our genders, sexualities, and social well-being.

Being involved, through assuming responsibilities for our cultures and societies, puts us in touch with the two remaining major broad social influences. For example, we become more responsible historical actors when we review our situations from the points of view of globalization as well as local communities. Similarly, when we make commitments to increase social justice, our motivations focus our attention on both local and global actions which are more responsible and more effective. Moreover, social justice ideals connect us to social realities in our cultures and societies, so that we can use socially intelligent principles to increase informed social justice goals.

Gender Fulfillment

Gender fulfillment flows from making responsible gender choices. Because gender fulfillment results from living fully, being responsible ensures that we are doing whatever we can to make the world more livable for more people. When we deliberately define our genders and identities, embrace our sexualities, and use our sexual orientations creatively, we make gender choices that are both responsible and fulfilling.

Social intelligence is a reliable guide in these ventures. We not only understand how important our genders, sexualities, and sexual orientations are in the total scheme of things, but we also use our awareness to express our genders in making better worlds. For example, we consider our genders in relation to the five major social influences of families, beliefs, social classes, cultures, and societies, so that we can control our behavior sufficiently to make decisions and commitments that increase the common good and social justice. We share what privileges we have, so that there are more opportunities for more people within and among our societies. We accomplish this by living according to social intelligence principles, which encourage us to examine social facts, to be objective, and to work with others who strive to achieve social justice values such as equality, inclusiveness, diversity, cooperation, and openness.

Our families are often sites of oppression rather than avenues of opportunity. Being socially intelligent means that we persist in seeing our families for what they are, and that we recognize their compelling forces toward conformity and emotional intensity. Similarly, our beliefs—which usually emerge historically through our families—need to be scrutinized and reviewed as major social influences in communities and globalization. We are responsible for the beliefs we choose to harbor and nurture, as well as for the consequences of our actions. Therefore, we need to discard as many of our unproductive beliefs as possible in order to live meaningfully, and to be fulfilled by working to achieve social justice goals.

As well as considering our genders, sexualities, and sexual orientations in our families and beliefs—and in trends of families and beliefs—we need to locate genders, sexualities, and sexual orientations in social classes. Much of the power that gender has over us results from social classes based on arbitrary distinctions about genders, sexualities, and sexual orientations. Social intelligence helps us to raise our gender class awareness sufficiently, in order to recognize why it is so difficult to change public attitudes that reinforce taboos about genders, sexualities, and sexual orientations. Social intelligence also motivates us to be more objective about social classes, so that we consider possibilities of classlessness in our thinking, actions, commitments, and social practices.

Fulfillment flows from recognizing how genders, sexualities, and sexual orientations influence social justice issues in families, beliefs, social classes, cultures, and societies. We examine some of the most important patterns of emotional dependency in these trends, for example, so that we lessen the intensity of their impacts on who we are, what we do, and how our cultures and societies affect globalization as well as interpersonal exchanges. In the same way that we examine families, beliefs, and social classes for inconsistencies, contradictions, and social injustices, we need to be aware of how our cultures and societies move us in both productive and destructive directions. We see how genders, sexualities, and sexual orientations influence our value choices, so that we can persevere in strengthening values that support social justice—such as equality, inclusiveness, diversity, cooperation, and openness.

When social justice guides us to apply social intelligence principles to families, beliefs, social classes, cultures, and societies, we are more likely to be fulfilled by our daily routines, as well as well as by accomplishing our goals. Genders, sexualities, and sexual orientations are important emotional resources that can contribute constructively to our collective efforts and fulfillment. Consequently, we need not be held back by genders, sexualities, and sexual orientations, but rather use these meaningful and powerful energies to express social justice in significant historical contexts that improve the lives of all.

From time to time, we review and sum up the extent to which we keep on track to accomplish our social justice goals, as well as our particular successes and failures in accomplishing these goals. For example, we try to maintain our objectivity and capacities to critique our efforts, so that we are more effective in attaining sound results. Furthermore, wherever possible we work with others to accomplish social justice, so that more people and more populations are fulfilled through their genders, sexualities, and sexual orientations.

Social Intelligence Expresses Gender

X. Emotional Interdependence and Gender

Genders are expressive aspects of our being and everyday life because they embody our deepest emotions. Intense emotions are both innate characteristics of human beings and the results of social taboos in conformity expectations about genders, sexualities, and sexual orientations. For example, our identities as individuals and human beings are called into question by our genders, especially when we become aware of our deepest yearnings, as well as the importance of our personal or public attachments.

Therefore, we cannot define or understand ourselves accurately unless we pay attention to the emotional aspects of who we believe we are, and how we interact in our closest relationships. Similarly, our gender identities, sexualities, and sexual orientations derive from deep emotional aspects of our being, whatever the specific genetic, biological, or physiological components of emotions are. For example, our families express patterns of interaction and interdependence that affect our emotions and actions in all aspects of our local or global behavior.

Our everyday associations with social classes are difficult to change, in part because we are emotionally resistant or emotionally insistent about such changes. Even without realizing the intensity of our emotional attachment to particular social class positions— for example, those social classes we think we are in, or those to which we aspire—our life courses and opportunities are affected by the rigidity of our social class bonds. Likewise our choices, responsibilities, and personal fulfillment flow from our attitudes to social class values in our cultures, as well as to dominant social class ways of doing things in our societies.

Social intelligence helps us to realize how life outcomes are connected to our emotional bonds with families, beliefs, social classes, cultures, and societies. For example, unless we see the influence of emotional interdependence in our genders, sexualities, and sexual orientations, we may not be able to loosen pernicious social bonds sufficiently to think clearly, and to commit ourselves to worthwhile projects about making constructive social changes for all. Our world views, as well as our personal lives, are subject to limitations in our capacities to deal with intense emotional entanglements in our everyday lives.

In some respects, social intelligence challenges us to undo critical ways in which we were socialized. For example, we need to discontinue patterns of interaction that reinforce problematic emotional interdependence. However, even though we cannot remove human needs to depend on others, we can become sufficiently independent in our thinking and actions to nurture increased objectivity about our life conditions and our most inspired goals. Furthermore, we cannot afford to stay tied to unproductive patterns of emotional interdependence with significant others, who may be either still living or dead. Creating conditions that support our freedom and autonomy are essential for meeting social justice goals to improve our families and societies.

Our focus on gender and social intelligence also suggests that we must detach ourselves from false dichotomies and rigid dualisms about genders, sexualities, and sexual orientations. Social intelligence shows us that human beings are more than either one sex or another sex. Rather, we must pay close attention to the complex broad ranges of differences in genders, sexualities, and sexual orientations that are the most meaningful and significant.

Creating better worlds for tomorrow means that we are prepared to deal effectively with diversity in our sexual behavior, and that societies adapt constructively to different ways of being and doing in expressing genders, sexualities, and sexual orientations. Consequently, we strengthen ourselves and others when we undertake tasks which focus on gender social issues in local and global everyday life.

Our starting points, in trajectories that bring about meaningful gender changes in individual and global situations, are to examine and understand emotional interdependence in the five major social influences of families, beliefs, social classes, cultures, and societies. Our capacities to be socially intelligent depend on our awareness of our emotional dependencies, and we increase our social intelligence primarily by taking charge of our deepest fears and concerns about survival, meaning, living fully, and being fulfilled.

Our most sublime moral ideals, as well as our most powerful positive or negative energies, are expressed as intense characteristics of our emotional interdependence. However, when we live according to social intelligence principles, we can choose to become sufficiently emotionally free to achieve some of our preferred life outcomes.

Gender Defined

Gender identities have significant impacts on the quality of life in societies, because our actions express our deepest emotional and social identities. Moreover, we create our own senses of identity when we are children, as well as when we are adults, which means that emotional interdependence continues to play a crucial part in how we see ourselves, others, and the world throughout our lives. In fact, emotional maturity is often hard-won, because all of us have tendencies to prolong or recreate our youthful emotional dependencies when we are adults, rather than deal effectively with the social issues of our original emotional interdependence.

One of the advantages of increasing our social intelligence is that we learn how to be both independent and emotionally interdependent. For example, we live more fully when we pay attention to our autonomy and freedom, while at the same time we acknowledge and respect our interdependence with others. Even though such a strategy often creates tensions in our relationships, this dynamic situation results from an unavoidable interplay of forces in being human and carving out our destinies. We are who we are partly because we are separate and different from others, and partly because we are very similar and close to them.

When we consider how to define gender identities in emotionally mature ways, we see that social intelligence enlightens and guides our views. We express ourselves with awareness of the push and pull of our emotional loyalties, at the same time that we try to remain true to ourselves and our intentions. Thus, we need to consider the most complex aspects of being a woman or being a man, for example, so that we do not oversimplify our understanding of what genders are or could be. No one can afford to be less than whole, so dichotomies of male and female are inappropriate guides to gender identities in the long run. Furthermore, only when we understand broad views of our lives can we grasp what it means to be a person who has gendered tendencies in thinking and acting. Our genders, in and of themselves, need not determine who we are and what we do.

Social intelligence nurtures our objectivity, and allows us to step back from some of the biological aspects of our sexualities that seem to direct our lives in important ways. Thus, we can question to what extent our genders fit our physiologies, or suggest directions that do not seem to be directly related to our genes. Although these broader views may sometimes lead us in conventional directions, our strengthened objectivity enables us to assess more easily the extent to which our sexualities and sexual orientations govern our actions, and whether this is more or less of what we want. Furthermore, socially intelligent objectivity enhances the options we see and identify with, because we define more clearly what our genders are for us and for others.

One finding of this scrutiny of our lives and social conditions in our societies is that we become increasingly aware of many everyday opportunities to define our genders, as well as the ways in which we allow others to define our genders. Social intelligence challenges the most dynamic aspects of our emotional interdependence, so that we become more emotionally mature and freer in defining our own genders. We express our genders maturely, rather than reactively, through using social intelligence, because social intelligence requires us to confront and deal with tensions between how we want to live our genders and what others expect of us as women or men.

When we use social intelligence to express the power and complexities of our genders, we do not reject gender responsibilities, but rather live up to them in more meaningful, effective ways. Being careful in defining genders helps us to make the world more just about gender, so that we can create further opportunities to express diverse genders. For example, when we are socially intelligent we spontaneously embrace diversity in genders, as well as create social conditions that support gender diversity.

Multifaceted definitions of genders, which emphasize how people are alike as well as how they are different, lead us in constructive directions toward building more just worlds for the future. We can only design progressive plans for populations when we have a clear understanding of the importance of social and emotional interdependence among and between women and men. Narrowing gender identities, and setting off one gender identity against another, creates unnecessary conflicts between gendered vested interests. By contrast, when we stay firmly based in our broadest thinking about social intelligence, gender identities, and social justice, we are more likely to produce just, gendered worlds now and in the future.

Gender and Sexuality

Because sexualities are critical components of genders, we must understand how taboos and controls over sexualities affect our genders. For example, history shows us that in most societies women have been valued primarily for their sexual and procreative powers, which were often feared by men as well as revered. However, in spite of the strength of the sexual and procreative influences that women have over men, women's lives were and often continue to be tightly restricted and narrowed by men's statuses, authority, and power. This historical trend, which is often very much a traditional social reality in less industrial societies, is also a source of varied taboos and controls about sexualities that continue to be found in modern societies.

In evolutionary terms it is only relatively recently that women have been sufficiently liberated, primarily through mass education, to assume more equal positions alongside men in modern societies. This is also because in times of war or economic strife, women have proved themselves to be effective, powerful partners in winning wars and supporting failing economies. Social intelligence builds on this knowledge of women's potentials and proven capacities for leadership. Sexualities become sources of energy for accomplishing chosen individual and social goals, rather than a rationale that men use to keep women in limited roles in societies and globalization.

One recurring theme, which must not be missed in this sketchy review of power relations between women and men, is that the emotional interdependence among women and among men is a powerful common denominator of their relationships, accomplishments, and possibilities. Throughout historical and evolutionary accounts of men's and women's survival strategies, the complementary functions of men and women have been over-emphasized. For example, these models and explanations are often based on men's protection of women as they bear children to meet personal and population needs. However, when discussions open up issues about qualities of life in civilizations, views of men and women as equals in existential terms take a stronger hold. Subsequently, trends among women—rather than individual exceptions—herald new ways to be considered equals in the power and complexities of modern societies and globalization.

The changing relationships of men and women are inevitably based on the continuing emotional interdependence between and among women and men. Emotional interdependence has consequences for female-male relations as well as for men's relationships with men and women's relationships with women. Both societies and civilizations are balanced, or thrown out of balance, by changing views of who women and men are, and by what they want to accomplish and do achieve in today's societies.

Social intelligence uses patterns of family interaction as a substantive base for understanding some the complex dynamics of emotional interdependence in genders and sexualities in societies and globalization. For example, we learn—through much pain and conflict—that women and men often respect each other more when each person takes advantage of opportunities to grow, has personal goals, and aims to meet national or international needs defined by the common good and social justice. Furthermore, to the extent that we act as though women and men are equal, they tend to become more equal in their relationships and particular situations. Equality between women and men in modern societies expresses emotional interdependence more freely than the more historic patterns of women and men in traditional subordinated relationships, that largely portray little more than men's power and control over women.

Social intelligence makes us more aware of existential necessities. For example, in order to survive in today's global world, as well as be fulfilled, we must make sufficient changes in value choices to usher in more just worlds. We are more productive, in increasing the common good and achieving social justice, when we cooperate with others to achieve equality, inclusiveness, diversity, and openness in our societies. These social conditions promote equality between women and men, which strengthens families and personal relationships as well as social accomplishments.

Social intelligence suggests that women and men will continue to react emotionally to each other over significant personal and social issues such as sexualities. However, to the extent that social intelligence gives us more control over our lives, we will tend to make new value choices that achieve more balanced relationships between women and men. Being socially intelligent is synonymous with encouraging and supporting opposite-sex or same-sex partners to have the same freedoms that we want for ourselves. Consequently, to the extent that we build egalitarian concerns into how to conduct ourselves successfully in our personal and public lives, we shall be more productive and more efficient in accomplishing social justice.

Gender and Sexual Orientation

Just as focusing on genders and sexualities is a social issue that has significant consequences for societies and globalization, genders and sexual orientations evoke concerns about the emotional interdependence between and among women and men. Issues about genders and sexual orientations often relate more directly to people's choices of sexual partners, which are at the core of sexualities and families in most modern societies.

It is in part because of the centrality of the social consequences of sexual orientations that genders and sexual orientations affect how we act in our most intimate exchanges, public communities, societies, and globalization. For example, when there are widespread disputes about genders and sexual orientations, the foundations of families and societies seem threatened. This occurs because well-established ways of dealing with the intense emotional interdependence of men and women are challenged at deep levels of being.

Thus, it is one thing for societies to allow criticisms of different expressions of sexualities in private and public arenas, and another to require any reorganization of sexualities through lifting taboos and restrictions about choices of sexual partners in temporary or lifetime commitments among women and men. For example, although we are compelled to reproduce ourselves as populations, as well as to express our sexualities, we must also respect the sexual traditions of different civilizations, and the basic ways in which societies have been and continue to be organized with regard to sexual behavior and families.

Social intelligence teaches us how to be open-minded and constructive in our thinking about social issues and social changes for better futures, which includes assessing and reassessing our sexual behavior and sexual orientations. For example, we must recognize emotional interdependence among all people, because we need to use thoughtful social reforms for institutional foundations that will not crumble. We need to learn how to withstand different sexual vested interests, as well as interpersonal and social conflicts about sexualities and genders. We educate ourselves about sexual diversity, so that we can implement social intelligence principles throughout populations. One of our collective goals continues to be to create social conditions that respect each person's sexual orientation amidst the power and complexities of social influences, societies, and globalization.

Social intelligence is founded on the emotional interdependence of our families because this is where we first learn—and constantly experience—the intensity of emotional interdependence among women and men. At best, we are strengthened by the emotional involvement and support of our families, so that we survive and also learn how to relate to others in the world. Ideally, we maintain contact with our families, and return to them, so that we stay vigorous or realistic in our views and experiences of emotional interdependence. This strengthens our knowledge of social facts about emotional interdependence, so that we understand more fully the depth of our conditioning in critical spheres of behavior such as sexual orientations.

Our socially intelligent knowledge of sexual orientations shows us how emotional interdependence and sexual orientations are found in wide ranges of individual and social behavior. We not only make sexual choices and express our sexualities in accordance with our sexual orientations, but we also perceive the world and act in ways that are strongly influenced by our sexual orientations. For example, we strengthen our understanding of the nature of human nature through our sexual orientations, and we decide how to commit our time and energies through sexual orientation choices. Consequently, there is no escape from our human frailties and strengths. We remain emotionally interdependent in our relations with others, especially through our most vulnerable sexualities and sexual orientations.

We use social intelligence principles to understand how to express our emotional interdependence constructively, in relations with people of different or similar sexual orientations. Being free in how we think and act, depends directly on the autonomy we create through our emotional dependence or independence in relation to others. Furthermore, unless we try to create social conditions that accept and support our emotional interdependence, we cannot harness our sexual energies sufficiently to control important aspects of our genders and sexual orientations. These are necessary preconditions that influence how effectively we create the improved worlds we yearn for today and for the future.

Gender Choices

Gender choices are consistently at the heart of the freedom we need to be our own real selves and to create our preferred communities and societies. Social intelligence increases our capacities to understand ourselves, communities, societies, and globalization, so that we make more authentic choices about our genders, sexualities, and sexual orientations. This does not mean that our private lives become public. Rather, we have greater peace of mind and willingness to make commitments to increase the common good and social justice, because we know considerably more social facts about who we are and what we want to accomplish. For example, we no longer play games of trying on many different identities for size, but rather aim to ring true through our decisions and actions, whatever our varied gender situations are.

The self awareness we gain from social intelligence principles, and our appreciation of the power and complexities of the five major social influences of families, beliefs, social classes, cultures, and societies, enable us to see and deal more effectively with the emotional interdependence of our genders. Our identities are not created in vacuums, so it is necessary to know how to see and take advantage of our gender choices through our emotional interdependence in a world of diverse genders, sexualities, and sexual orientations. For example, we must be sufficiently courageous to continue to carve out our gendered selves, whatever our situations are, if we are to be socially intelligent about our gender choices now and throughout our lives.

X. Emotional Interdependence and Gender

The omnipresence of our emotional interdependence means that we must maintain clarity about our priorities and goals in order to achieve them. For example, our emotional interdependence manifests itself in many different ways, which include the push and pull of social pressures to conform to others' preferences and expectations. Ironically, those who are nearest and dearest to us are often the most demanding in their pressures to conform to particular expectations. Therefore, we must know how to negotiate with them effectively when we make our gender choices, and when we decide to become more socially intelligent. We must also meet and deal with others' resistance and opposition when they disagree with what we think we need and want as our highest priorities.

Overall, we essentially choose only whether to accept or reject our gender choices, as well as whether to accept or reject our emotional interdependence. Whatever our decisions and commitments are, these choices cost us most dearly when we deny our gender choices and deny our emotional interdependence. For example, when we reject our gender choices we become markedly less socially intelligent in each decision and commitment we make. We are also considerably less realistic and objective when we reject our emotional interdependence, because emotional interdependence is a basic and essential part of who we are as human beings. We are only truly responsible—which usually results in increased gender fulfillment—when we cultivate our most meaningful gender choices, as well as when we educate ourselves about the power and complexities of our emotional interdependence in the five major social influences of families, beliefs, social classes, cultures, and societies.

Seeing our emotional interdependence and gender choices through social justice is a major advantage and opportunity of being socially intelligent. Our social intelligence gives us broad perspectives, such as social justice, which allow us to see the most significant social realities of our lives knowingly, and to act accordingly. We live with more clearly defined purpose and direction when we are socially intelligent, so that we can unsnarl some of life's problems more effectively, and move on constructively to create better societies for today and tomorrow. Gender choices open up our lives, and motivate us to reduce the restrictiveness of conventional thinking and acting about genders.

Constructive gender choices include examining what we do in our families, beliefs, social classes, cultures, and societies. For example, how do we exercise our gender choices in our families? To what extent do we practice free expressions of our genders in our families? How do gender beliefs restrict our thinking about genders and social justice? Which of these beliefs must we change in order to have more authenticity in our gender choices? How do our social classes impinge on our gender choices? To what extent are our genders restricted by being social classes in their own right? Do our cultures reinforce or limit our gender freedoms? How do cultures clarify our gender choices and emotional interdependence? To what extent do societies reveal or hide our emotional interdependence? How does emotional interdependence influence our established ways of doing things in societies?

Gender Responsibilities

Social intelligence guides us to make responsible gender choices, especially with regard to our most deep-seated emotional interdependence. Because emotional interdependence motivates many of our most reactive thoughts and actions, social intelligence serves to protect us from their hazardous consequences, and essentially neutralizes them. In these respects, being responsible by increasing our social intelligence prevents us from wasting our talents and energies in unproductive actions.

Although social intelligence can be used for evil ends, the focus of *Social Intelligence and Gender* is exclusively on the optimal outcomes of social intelligence in everyday life and public social issues. We also consider that gender responsibilities mean those socially intelligent actions which empower self for good purposes, such as increasing the common good and social justice.

X. Emotional Interdependence and Gender

For example, when we understand the power and complexities of the five major social influences of families, beliefs, social classes, cultures, and societies, we are at the same time aware of needs for enlightened socially intelligent decisions, strategies, and commitments to improve social conditions for all, in order to survive and be fulfilled in our emotional interdependence.

When our gender responsibilities aim to balance emotional interdependence in social relations more effectively, they are more likely to usher in better worlds, ensure more beneficial legacies, and increase gender fulfillment. We take different stepping-stones to increase our social intelligence, so that we balance our emotional interdependence as well as achieve socially intelligent goals. When we are aware of our genders, gender identities, sexualities, sexual orientations, and gender choices, we deliberately select gender responsibilities that address emotional interdependence and achieve socially intelligent goals.

In these ways social intelligence guides us to participate in chains of constructive social reactions and social possibilities, so that we knowingly play significant parts in improving social conditions in our gendered emotional interdependence in societies and the world. For example, we realize that we are key players—as responsible historical actors—in creating more equality, inclusiveness, diversity, cooperation, and openness in civilizations of today and tomorrow. We work with others to accomplish worthwhile goals that make life more livable for those who are oppressed and cannot act on their own behalf.

Our value choices in our everyday lives inevitably have major constructive consequences for unborn generations. Socially meaningful visions of better worlds inspire people to address their ongoing emotional interdependence needs, so that they take more enlightened actions that show members of the next generation how to apply principles of social intelligence in their everyday lives. Thus, our value choices are significant influences in present and future worlds. Consequently, one of our primary gender responsibilities is the extent to which we incorporate gender sensitivities and gender concerns into our gender choices and emotional interdependence. For example, at the same time that we carve out emotional freedom to make improved gender choices, we increase gender fulfillment for ourselves and others.

When we develop sufficient social intelligence about our genders, sexualities, and sexual orientations, we become historical actors who are headed in responsible gender directions. For example, historical actors take emotional interdependence into account as primary, compelling social conditions in planning and implementing actions to change genders. Even though we know that we want to eventually accomplish responsible gender goals, merely working toward these ends is often enough for now. As long as we try to achieve more mature emotional interdependence through aiming at responsible gender goals, we know that we are doing as much as we can do now to meet our gender responsibilities. In these respects, we actively journey with others toward improved worlds, which address gender needs and emotional interdependence in our civilizations as well as our interpersonal behavior.

Some of the specific changes that derive from assuming gender responsibilities include questioning existing gender roles in our families, and developing new ways to relate to our relatives. We also critically assess our most deep-seated beliefs about genders, sexualities, and sexual orientations, so that we are more consistent in our gendered actions and emotional interdependence. For example, we challenge gender beliefs that support gendered social classes, so that we can forge ways that break out of the social subordinations of genders, sexualities, and sexual orientations in our emotional interdependence. We also deliberately examine our cultures, so that we make new value choices that guide our genders to create more socially intelligent changes in emotional interdependence, societies, and civilizations.

Gender Fulfillment

In some respects, issues about emotional interdependence persist, regardless of any of the specific individual and social changes we may make through pursuing responsible gender goals.

X. Emotional Interdependence and Gender

For example, even though we may consider that we are emotionally mature, there are always challenges that tempt us to give up our emotional freedoms, so that we continue to conform to others' goals and expectations rather than achieve our own. However, unless we focus on our own gender responsibilities as motivations and actions, we cannot increase our gender fulfillment.

Social intelligence shows us that we need to create and maintain social conditions that enable more people to make new value choices, if we are to achieve gender fulfillment. Because genders are a core aspect of who we are, we must scrutinize how we define our genders, sexualities, and sexual orientations in current, historical, and cultural settings. This sharpens our awareness of how we choose constructive social values—such as equality, inclusiveness, diversity, cooperation, and openness—to increase the common good and social justice. Such clarity allows us to act more responsibly, so that we achieve fulfillment, as well as specific goals that increase the common good and social justice.

We cannot afford to turn our backs on the importance of ethical and existential concerns as we work with others to improve social well-being. For example, we need to be aware of the power and complexities of social influences, at the same time that social intelligence shows us ways to motivate us and others to achieve far-reaching goals which improve social situations for all. Social intelligence also shows us that we need to cultivate meaningful directions in our lives, in order to resolve some of the individual and social ethical or existential dilemmas we face each day. Therefore, both our survival and fulfillment depend on applying social intelligence principles in our private and public lives.

The emotional interdependence of our gendered beings requires that we give close attention to gender, sexuality, and sexual orientation issues in our decision-making and commitments. For example, we honor the social significance of genders, sexualities, and sexual orientations at the same time that we examine the five major social influences of families, beliefs, social classes, cultures, and societies. This allows social intelligence to clarify important substantive details in how we interact with these five major social influences, so that we are more responsible in designing goals and making commitments to achieve them.

Gender fulfillment results from recognizing our emotional interdependence in our families, beliefs, social classes, cultures, and societies. However, there are no short cuts to achieve gender fulfillment, because we are compelled to act on our current understanding and awareness of the complex social foundations of our genders, sexualities, and sexual orientations. For example, we must realize the extent to which our actions are more effective when we work with like-minded others, and when we create social justice conditions to improve the situations of all.

Emotional interdependence is a given in both individual and social human situations. We cannot resolve emotional dependency issues so that they are no longer significant, but rather we aspire to increase our emotional maturity, so that we protect ourselves from being immediately drawn into strong flows of cultural fads and foibles against our wills. Emotional freedom and maturity enable us to see our social conditions more objectively and more accurately, so that we can use social intelligence principles to create visions that propel us toward better futures.

This does not mean that our emotional interdependence is a situational hazard that must be avoided. Rather, we benefit from appreciating emotional interdependence as a constructive and powerful resource, that at best may serve the common good. For example, we use our knowledge of emotional interdependence to shed light on the depth of our gender, sexuality, and sexual orientation conditioning, so that we make wiser decisions and more realistic commitments to bring about effective strategic changes. We see that women and men, as well as homosexual and heterosexual people, have strong emotional interdependence, which has the potential to either impede or propel their progress toward creating improved societies. Therefore, our civilizations depend on expressing our emotional interdependence in meaningful and strategic ways, so that we are more fully human and humane to each other because of our emotional interdependence.

XI. The Common Good and Gender

Our genders, sexualities, and sexual orientations affect, and are impacted by, the five major social influences of families, beliefs, social classes, cultures, and societies as well as the common good. This happens because how we interact with others depends in part on how our societies and globalization are organized, and which social forces define social changes in these broad aspects of our being. The power and complexities of societies and globalization are more than contexts or external influences, because they are experienced as internal guides in our personal and social existential conditions. Therefore, it is imperative that we come to terms with these influences if we are to define our own destinies, and create future societies based on a common good.

Because we are emotionally interdependent in our relations with each other, the reciprocity of genders, sexualities, sexual orientations, societies, and globalization provides resources that we can choose to use, rather than powers to which we must passively succumb. Social intelligence requires us to question the wide variety of social contexts we enter into each day, so that we can then move more freely in directions that give us some control over our decisions, commitments, and actions. For example, we see more clearly how to design alternative futures, and realize that we must create more constructive social conditions for the years to come, if we are to survive and be fulfilled.

Gender is an anchor point that makes tremendous differences to the quality of life for individuals, communities, societies, and globalization. When we question deeply what our genders mean, and how we identify our gender responsibilities, our usual patterns of behavior can be turned around slowly and societies gradually reoriented. Even though it is both difficult and challenging to make radical changes in how we deal with our genders, sexualities, and sexual orientations, we benefit from letting these critical aspects of our being become direct inspirations for how we define the common good, and how we take responsible action to increase the common good.

Moving in these directions need not be a lonely endeavor. Social intelligence encourages us to work cooperatively with like-minded others, so that we make meaningful changes in social conditions that affect us all. In these respects we may choose to transform our most personal spheres of social relations, so that we become historical actors who participate more deliberately in social forces and widespread currents of changes in societies and globalization. By being whoever we are with respect to our genders, sexualities, and sexual orientations we can impact others as well as ourselves, increase our social intelligence, and act more effectively to enrich the common good.

Participating in ongoing complex social changes connects our genders to history and meaningful social goals. At the same time that we continue to increase our working knowledge of societies, we use broad perspectives to guide us in whatever we do. Consequently, social intelligence is expressed more effectively in our emotionally interdependent actions with others. Our greater depth of understanding helps us to visualize new dimensions of the common good, so that we are both creative and innovative in formulating goals that increase the common good and social justice.

In some respects seeking to expand the common good is both similar to but different from aiming to achieve social justice goals. The common good is often experienced as a simpler, shorter-term objective than social justice, because it is easier to think about the common good in relation to small groups rather than globalization. Furthermore, because it is often simpler to design and implement goals to increase the common good rather than social justice in our everyday lives, we are often more specific about how gender issues relate to the common good in our communities. For example, we more easily know how new local legislation could alter the living conditions of people with minority sexual orientations in our own towns, when they are having difficulty in establishing their families.

Thus, the common good gives us a meaningful purpose and direction to pursue, which balances our emotional interdependence productively, through creating living conditions that move us toward equality, inclusiveness, diversity, cooperation, and openness. Even though we may not necessarily be successful in achieving our common good goals, moving in these constructive directions helps us to connect our genders, sexualities, and sexual orientations to historical missions that increase the common good and social justice.

Gender Defined

How we define our genders and gender identities inevitably influences the quality of our contributions to the common good. For example, we can only accomplish what we think we are capable of, and what we understand the consequences of our actions are. In order to be well-intentioned in increasing the common good, we must know what our genders mean, and how our actions impact us and our societies.

Social intelligence and achieving the common good depend on seeing who we are in relation to families, beliefs, social classes, cultures, and societies. When we make genders our starting points for understanding the power and complexities of social influences in our lives, we see that our definitions of genders vary. Furthermore, the consequences of our actions depend directly on how we define genders. For example, exploring the historical origins of genders through our families deepens our individual understanding of the importance of defining genders, and suggests socially intelligent ways to change our genders when our families' definitions of gender are too narrow or unrealistic.

Similarly, we examine our beliefs in our relationships and societies, in order to discover how gender is incorporated and perpetuated through our beliefs, and how our beliefs affect the common good. Changing inappropriately restrictive beliefs about genders is usually best accomplished by exploring their diverse historical origins—such as our families, schools, and cultures—so that we interact differently now, which gradually modifies our basic gender definitions and their impacts on our thinking and actions for achieving the common good.

One of the more hidden aspects of defining gender results from whether or not we are aware of social classes, and of how gender is a significant social class in its own right in most traditional and modern societies. When we use social intelligence to recognize and understand gendered differences in resources, education, power, agency, and values, we realize more fully what the consequences of particular gender identity contrasts are for achieving the common good, and how we need to increase opportunities for disadvantaged genders or sexual social classes in our societies. For example, social intelligence teaches us that gendered social classes are not innate and can be changed at any time, especially when both women and men work together to increase the common good.

Our definitions of gender also evolve from our cultures. We often experience the dominance of our family cultures as children, but sooner or later—especially through education—we open up our family cultures, in order to incorporate influences from other cultures in our everyday behavior, and to achieve a common good. Social intelligence helps us to recognize the power and complexities of cultural nuances in genders, as well as the options that different cultures offer in defining genders. For example, complementary characteristics of being female or male are frequently exaggerated in some cultures, with the result that we may lose sight of the importance of cultivating a common good that benefits all genders and all sexual orientations. Therefore, we need to examine carefully the many ways in which cultural values reinforce or challenge our own gender values, so that we can more effectively stop ourselves from perpetuating pernicious and dysfunctional gender inequalities.

When we have sufficient social intelligence to become responsible historical actors, we understand more fully how our societies have defined genders and sexes through time, and what the negative and positive consequences of these definitions are for the common good. When we use social intelligence to solve social issues and increase the common good as historical actors, we necessarily work toward changing destructive gender definitions, so that more people free themselves from these restrictive ways of thinking and acting. For example, at best societies help to spread education throughout their own societies and other countries in the context of globalization, so that more of their citizens and world citizens open up and enhance their gendered social destinies to benefit the common good.

Social intelligence guides our expressions of gender through requiring us to reassess our individual and shared gender definitions. When we see complex nuances in histories of our gender identities and the common good, we are more likely to change our definitions of genders in the present for the future. In fact, we may achieve better futures only when we pay attention to socially intelligent ways to approach and define genders and gender issues, as well as the common good.

Whatever we choose to use as basic definitions of genders are powerful determinants of our behavior and social conditions. Considering the common good as our central purpose in revising our gender definitions, gives us hope for improving gender and sexual relations in the present and future. For example, constructive changes in conventional gender definitions deepen respect between men and women, as well as draw attention to the importance of making value choices to support equality, inclusiveness, diversity, cooperation, and openness for the common good.

Gender and Sexuality

Sexualities have histories and characteristics which affect the common good, especially when we consider the social consequences of cultural taboos about sexualities. Also, because moral concerns are often at the heart of cultural taboos, sexualities are unceasingly subjected to close scrutiny through the moral views and attitudes of mainstream societies. Consequently, sexual habits and practices that go beyond or against conventional standards of moral and cultural behavior, are often stigmatized through prejudice and discrimination.

Social intelligence shows us that juxtaposing our needs to increase the common good with needs to express genders and sexualities helps us to find ways to balance these needs constructively, especially when social conditions do not reflect socially intelligent values such as equality, inclusiveness, diversity, cooperation, and openness. Moreover, when we persist in aiming to achieve a common good that increases social justice, we eventually reach a more effective balance among our diverse needs.

Another socially intelligent route to create a practical balance in our needs is to look at genders and sexualities within and among our families, beliefs, social classes, cultures, and societies. This strategy grounds our ideals and aspirations in social realties more firmly. For example, we deepen our understanding of emotional needs by examining social facts in our families, which include repeated patterns of behavior around genders and sexualities. Similarly, we learn from social facts in beliefs, social classes, cultures, and societies, which also reveal wide ranges of distinctive patterns of behavior around genders and sexualities. Consequently, increasing our social intelligence and social know-how prepares us to do whatever it takes to design effective goals for creating a common good that reflects the needs of all genders and sexualities.

Considering our families links our awareness of emotional interdependence to achieving a multifaceted common good. In many respects families behave according to emotional pressures in their communities, as well as in relation to emphases in their present and past generations. When we change patterns of prejudice and discrimination in our families, we create new social conditions that support gender and sexual diversity in families, communities, and the common good. For example, recognizing social rejection and cultural taboos enables us to increase opportunities to express genders, sexualities, and the common good more freely.

XI. The Common Good and Gender

We also need to examine our individual, family, and community beliefs about genders and sexualities. Our most powerful opinions create attitudes that motivate us, or restrict us, with regard to initiating or resisting changes that increase the common good. For example, social intelligence guides us to nurture our most constructive beliefs, so that we gradually replace destructive beliefs that block progress, by creating social conditions to increase the common good. When we believe in possibilities for a better future, where diversity in beliefs about genders and sexualities is embraced and incorporated in socially established ways of doing things, we start to achieve a more widely shared common good and social justice.

Some of the strife among genders and sexualities exists because different genders and sexualities are social classes. Genders and sexualities or sexual orientations are social classes in their own right, which may support or resist change to increase the common good. For example, established hierarchies of genders and sexualities often comfort people because they are familiar. By contrast, when we challenge the status quo by equalizing cultural or social resources among genders and sexualities, social discomfort or unrest is often experienced.

In addition, our cultures may serve as sources of inspiration for new social adaptations around genders and sexualities in achieving the common good. Because there are many valid ways to increase the common good, we find constructive opportunities to develop genders and sexualities as new cultural ideals that incorporate equality, inclusiveness, diversity, cooperation, and openness. When these new ideals become value choices among individuals and populations, grass root shifts in how people think and express their genders or sexualities occur. These adaptations are critical aspects of broad national and global changes in attitudes about genders, sexualities, and major social influences in societies, at the same time that they increase the common good.

Because social intelligence inspires gender and sexuality changes in families, beliefs, social classes, and cultures, historical actors are encouraged to increase the common good of societies and civilizations. Thus, they benefit from focusing on the broadest perspectives of sexualities and globalization, at the same time that they deal with local concerns. Maintaining this wide vision helps us to create and maintain a common good that encourages freedom of expression for diverse genders and sexualities. Ideally, when sexualities are accepted more widely, genders become more authentic, and social justice flows from a reinvigorated common good.

Gender and Sexual Orientation

Populations accept diverse sexualities when they are able to embrace more differences in sexual orientations. Populations that want to establish and maintain a universal common good must create and support social conditions that express diverse genders, sexualities, and sexual orientations, as well as social justice values such as equality, inclusiveness, diversity, cooperation, and openness. Thus knowledge about genders is a catalyst which opens up families, communities, and societies that were previously closed to considering varieties of genders, sexualities, and sexual orientations as significant aspects of the common good.

We need to make room for wide ranges of sexual behaviors in both our traditional and modern societies because being free is a central component of social intelligence. For example, when populations create some flexibility in their moral norms and standards, individuals and groups are more able to choose how to express their sexualities and sexual orientations. Establishing freedom of choice for all in relation to genders, sexualities, and sexual orientations should not offend mainstream moral standards, but rather protect minority sexualities. In these ways, social intelligence principles guide us to achieve a balanced common good that increases gender, sexuality, and sexual orientation possibilities for more people in more populations.

Focusing on both genders and sexual orientations gives us new views of the five major social influences of families, beliefs, social classes, cultures, and societies. For example, seeing emotional interdependence in our families helps us to understand how sexual orientations tend to be taken for granted rather than accepted as individual or social preferences. We need to help family members with minority sexual orientations to live authentically and pursue the common good within or outside our families, rather than allow the prejudice and discrimination of relatives to pressure them to conform to questionable family standards of sexual orientation.

We must also understand how the behavior of people with varied sexual orientations evokes inaccurate and ignorant beliefs about sexual orientations. As socially intelligent mature adults, we continuously edit and revise our beliefs, so that we become more deliberate in our understanding of sexual orientation realities. For example, social intelligence makes us particularly aware of the power of social influences in increasing negative prejudices and discrimination, as well as in producing positive values and commitments. This helps us to take charge of our beliefs about sexual orientations, so that we ensure that we act to expand the common good through our gendered actions and goals.

Social classes often hide the extent to which our attitudes about how we think and what we do are influenced by established social hierarchies. For instance, we may be slow to admit that social classes are created by varied sexual orientations, with homosexual social classes usually having less power and prestige than heterosexual social classes. However, these social classes can be changed, especially if new legislation is used to expand the common good, by ensuring specific individual and social rights for people with minority sexual orientations. As with other aspects of learned behavior, social intelligence guides us to change unjust social classes, whatever the social bases of our social classes are, because such inequities block achievement of the common good.

In modern times, cultures are primary sources of knowledge and symbols that describe or explain minority sexual orientations and the common good. For example, our cultures educate us about critical differences in bisexual or transsexual orientations. Similarly we learn from our cultures and formal education how homosexual families have similar patterns of emotional interdependence as heterosexual families, although sometimes these patterns are more intense in homosexual families, due to external pressures from community prejudices and discrimination.

Social intelligence uses historical perspectives to understand societal dynamics in sexual orientations and the common good. We often accept homosexual orientations more, for example, when we assess the extent to which societies embraced genders and sexualities in different historical times, and how people with homosexual orientations were required to cope with societies' prejudice and discrimination, sometimes to the point of threatened death or death. It is partly due to the intensity of our emotional interdependence and the strength of our urges to conform—in order to feel as though we are wanted members of societies—that cultural taboos continue to cluster around sexual orientations in different societies through time.

We focus more effectively on increasing the common good when we are knowledgeable about how the five major social influences of families, beliefs, social classes, cultures, and societies impact our sexual orientations. At the same time, we are often affected by the negative power of these major social influences, unless we deliberately use social intelligence and social justice to guide us to increase the common good. Cultivating broad viewpoints makes us more responsible historical actors, and we achieve more social justice when we expand the common good.

Gender Choices

Once we are aware of the significance and consequences of making gender choices, we are more likely to invest our actions in creating improved futures by increasing the common good. Identifying with our genders, as well as transcending our genders, opens up our gender choices because we experience being at one with both particular genders and all humankind. Having this breadth of vision about the nature of human nature, frees us to articulate goals which go beyond the emotional dictates of our particular situations. For example, social intelligence guides us to continue to make wise gender choices, so that we increase the common good and benefit others as well as ourselves.

We scrutinize our own families, families in our communities, family trends in societies, and families in globalization in order to understand and assess the extent to which behaviors are driven by emotional needs rather than thoughtful goals. For example, we are sometimes pressured into particular dependencies in our families, so that we use our energies primarily to react to or recycle our families' patterns of emotional interdependence, rather than meet and deal with difficult social situations constructively.

However, when we run into obstacles in dealing with the emotional limitations of our beliefs, social classes, cultures, and societies, we benefit from reconnecting with our families, in order to become stronger. This happens because we can more easily reassess our social intelligence and common good goals in the context of our families' emotional interdependence.

In the same way that families serve us as prisms to see who we are and how we understand or select our options, our gender choices are also influenced by our beliefs. We set limits about who we are through our genders, by our acceptance and rejection of particular beliefs about genders. When we use social intelligence and the common good to guide our thinking, motivation, actions, and commitments, we become more deliberate in focusing on our most constructive beliefs, in order to let go of beliefs about gender which limit our world views. Realizing wide ranges of options in this way gradually enriches our contributions to the common good, especially in relation to our social justice missions to enlarge our gender limits.

As we loosen our choices by exploring families and beliefs, we scrutinize the remaining social influences of social classes, cultures, and societies more effectively. Even though the breadth of perspectives on social classes, cultures, and societies may seem to have more direct impacts in opening up our gender choices, we all too easily strive to conform to others' agendas, or to maintain the status quo. We often have vested interests in our own social classes, for example, so that in spite of our budding gender awareness, we may decide to follow lines of action governed by limited gender choices. When we clarify our allegiances to one sexual orientation, whatever that orientation is, we tend to narrow our gender and sexual choices, with the result that we do not strive for a general common good, but rather seek to protect and expand the interests of small groups in communities and societies.

Thus, our gender choices may express vested interests in our cultures, rather than constructive cultural values that reflect a universal common good. For example, cultures may reinforce social class hierarchies, because they express differences in education—or social class contrasts—which inevitably underlie what most people understand as their cultures. Consequently, our gender value choices may either motivate us to support existing gender restrictions, or free us from narrow gender definitions. When we use our social intelligence to assess our options, we see more clearly that we thrive from pursuing value choices such as equality, inclusiveness, diversity, cooperation, and openness, because they confirm common good goals and social justice.

Societies give us advantageous broad views of our everyday lives, as well as help us to understand that we participate in global trends today for the future. It is particularly sobering, but rewarding, to learn about national and international current affairs—if only from reading serious newspapers—so that we are gradually compelled to understand our gender choices in terms of complex international dynamics. We view our gender choices differently with these wide-angle lenses, and we use our social intelligence and common good guides to define our gender responsibilities and gender fulfillment through our most meaningful gender choices.

Gender Responsibilities

When we consistently use broad perspectives to consider our gender options, we become more responsible for the consequences of our actions. For example, we address what we and our families need, and at the same time try to understand and act on our socially intelligent awareness of globalization, including the needs of others as well as our own. Because we use broad views to assess social realities and the common good, we confront and deal more responsibly with existential issues about our meanings and purposes to live, as well as how genders relate to these social contexts.

Ideally, we strive to be socially intelligent at all times. This means that we use our working knowledge of the five major social influences of families, beliefs, social classes, cultures, and societies to come to terms with our emotional interdependence and our needs to increase the common good. We are enlightened activists in our own social situations, and we refuse to be pressured into following the dictates of others' narrow agendas. Our broad world views and attitudes motivate us to pursue the common good responsibly, rather than follow only the ambitions of our narrow self interests.

We focus our attention on genders, sexualities, and sexual orientations so that we can improve social conditions around these issues, and create a more viable common good. Maintaining socially intelligent views of general purposes in our everyday lives gives us clarity about the many applications and implications that genders, sexualities, and sexual orientations have for qualities of life in society. For example, we understand more fully the significance of using the common good as a foundation or springboard for changing these vital social conditions.

Our value choices, decisions, and commitments are more responsible when we engage in reassessing our priorities, so that we continue to increase the common good more effectively. Although it is always imperative to recognize individual differences, we use the social intelligence principle that the whole is more than the sum of the parts as a guide. This helps us to see that each of us must give back to the groups we depend on the most, in order to be responsible and universal in our thinking and actions. We are social beings because the five major social influences of families, beliefs, social classes, cultures, and societies have created who we are, as well as the limits of what we can do. However, our deepest freedom comes from committing ourselves to give back to the common good or social justice, by expressing our awareness that our lives are more than our genders, sexualities, sexual orientations, families, beliefs, social classes, cultures, and societies.

Responsible actions result from cultivating socially intelligent awareness, making meaningful commitments, and gaining results from our intentions and goals. We know that these accomplishments are often the stuff of dreams, and may not have dared to dwell on such lofty ideals. Nevertheless, because the principles of social intelligence include selecting new values to guide us, we incorporate them in responsible actions that deal effectively with social realities and increase the common good. For example, issues about genders, sexualities, and sexual orientations are among the most difficult dilemmas we need to settle for our individual and social well-being, so that we can focus more on achieving the common good.

When we examine what really goes on in our families, we find that responsibility often includes doing unpleasant chores so that families can function well. Also, in spite of the delights of family intimacies and love, we must realize that families have dark sides, and may be destructive rather than constructive influences in our lives. Given these contradictions, being responsible requires that we face up to whatever the facts are of our given family situations. This means that we are not content to build myths or rosy ideals that camouflage the uncomfortable emotional dependency issues of families, genders, sexualities, sexual orientations, and the common good.

When we use the common good as a primary direction for our decision-making, and ground our strategies in social intelligence principles, we are responsible in our intentions and actions in the long run. A goal of increasing the common good helps us to express socially intelligent values such as equality, inclusiveness, diversity, cooperation, and openness more creatively and more universally. This shows that we are on track to achieve the common good and social justice, even though previously these aims may have seemed unrealistic or unattainable.

184

XI. The Common Good and Gender

Gender Fulfillment

In some respects gender fulfillment is produced by the peace of mind we experience from expressing our gender responsibilities. We also gain gender fulfillment by participating in projects that are bigger than ourselves, which aim to achieve constructive social goals, such as increasing the common good or social justice. For example, when we know that we are doing all we can in the present to accomplish better futures, we continue to become socially intelligent through meeting our gender responsibilities.

Because living according to socially intelligent principles guides us to become more fulfilled in expressing our genders, we pay attention to social facts and historical world views in our thinking and actions. We formulate strategies to give us some control over the strongest social influences of families, beliefs, social classes, cultures, and societies, in order to maintain a sufficiently astute awareness of our effectiveness in these social spheres of personal and public priorities. This encourages us to be responsible global historical actors, who use their gender resources to increase the common good.

Social intelligence is a valuable asset in this long term process. Even though we cannot change all social conditions around gender issues during our lifetimes, we can persist in progressing in these directions. Defining and working with others toward common good goals about genders is a creative and productive way to invest our gender energies. Being examples of how to express our genders constructively shows others the importance of social intelligence principles in everyday life.

Perhaps one of the main messages we need to communicate about genders is the often unrealized ways in which genders define or control our lives. Just as we express the importance of social intelligence through our actions, we may also point out how genders can make or break our lives when we do not understand the power and complexities of major social influences. For example, unless we are vigilant and astute in expressing gendered values in our social situations, we lose control in defining who we are and what we want to accomplish for the common good.

In order to increase our gender fulfillment, we must assess and continue to evaluate the social impacts of the five major social influences of families, beliefs, social classes, cultures, and societies. Our existential awareness also suggests that we need to use our minds, rather than abuse or ignore our intellectual capacities, so that we can map out an enriched common good. For example, we consider universal concerns about the common good when we apply social intelligence principles to understanding families, beliefs, social classes, cultures, and societies.

Gender fulfillment results from taking our emotional interdependence seriously in relation to achieving the common good. We experience emotional behavior in our families and assess how family dependencies influence who we are and what we do. Furthermore, when we consistently try to be mature and independent in our families, we become more effective in achieving the common good in other social settings. For example, we assume family responsibilities, so that we meet the real needs of relatives and others' families. Also, because families yield vital information about who we are and how we need to resolve our emotional dependencies, we examine family histories to discover both our vulnerabilities and our strengths.

We also increase gender fulfillment and the common good when we scrutinize our gender beliefs, and resolve contradictions and conflicts in our beliefs. For example, we may decide to discard strong emphases in others' gender beliefs which influenced us historically. Tackling dubious aspects of our gender beliefs at their sources gives us more control over how we consider the common good now, whether we absorbed our beliefs from families, education, religions, politics, or cultures. Because we are emotionally dependent on others, we regain our autonomy by being more objective about our beliefs, so that we deliberately develop new emphases for the future.

Similarly social classes, including gender social classes, may block our gender fulfillment and achievement of the common good. We examine whether gendered social classes predispose us to use all our energies, for example, in order to reject any restrictive dominance that gendered social classes wield over our thinking and acting. This lifetime project has many significant nuances which may not be known until the future. However, we increase our gender fulfillment now merely by realizing how gendered social classes define or restrict the freedom of both women and men to achieve the common good.

Our cultures are other influences on our capacities to accomplish gender fulfillment and the common good. Being caught up in conventional values and priorities often deadens our abilities to discern subtle gender symbols and values in our cultures. When we live according to social intelligence principles, however, we use social intelligence to guide us through the confusing mazes of our cultures based on values, ideas, ideals, education, legal systems, religions, and social expectations for genders, sexualities, and sexual orientations. Social intelligence principles help us to assess the constructiveness or destructiveness of our cultures, so that we choose common good and social justice values—equality, inclusiveness, diversity, cooperation, and openness—to enhance our gender fulfillment.

The last chapter of *Social Intelligence and Gender*, **History and Gender**, gives a detailed account of how societies—the fifth major social influence that has significant impacts on social intelligence—yield gender fulfillment and an increased common good. The broad perspective of societies also gives us a fuller understanding of how social intelligence transforms some qualities of our day-to-day lives, so that we accomplish a more viable common good and gender fulfillment.

XII. History and Gender

Society is the broadest social perspective from which to view the common good, history, and gender in globalization. When we understand how societies are organized, particularly through their complex patterns of emotional interdependencies, we realize the significance of major social influences—such as families, beliefs, social classes, cultures, and societies—in impacting who we are and what we do. Social intelligence directs our capacities to use this basic knowledge to make constructive changes in how we conduct ourselves individually and collectively each day.

At best, the common good becomes a preferred goal as we deepen our socially intelligent understanding of history and gender. As human beings we benefit from achieving goals which provide meanings for how we live, how we make decisions, and how we establish priorities in goals. Having purposes such as increasing our social intelligence, achieving a common good, and enhancing social justice also requires values and objectives which show us how to live history more fully. For example, knowing we are responsible for making changes in how we do things and how societies accomplish their business ultimately enhances our well-being and gender fulfillment.

Social intelligence wakens us to these possibilities. Whereas we might have previously thought that we were not sufficiently worthy to have goals such as being an historical actor, or aiming to increase the common good, we see now that this is what we must do in order to survive and be fulfilled. For example, we cannot hope to understand gender merely intellectually. We must live our genders deliberately by making changes in our minds and actions, because this is how we live more deeply.

When we define our genders in light of history—what has been and what is now happening in our societies—we see that our experiences of gender are not only our most intimate and personal dimensions of being, but also ways in which we interact publicly and historically with others. There is no escape from these social facts, or from our ethical responsibilities as human beings. We all need to participate directly in defining the nature of human nature. Furthermore, although as humans we have choices, there are inevitable consequences of being human and being gendered.

This way of thinking leads to the assumption that we are primarily social beings. Consequently, we benefit from learning and applying principles of social intelligence to ourselves and others in whatever we think or do, and we start to change ourselves and others by seeing the most significant social influences in our lives differently. For example, we understand our emotional interdependence with others more fully when we see how people interact with five of the strongest emotional influences in our lives—families, beliefs, social classes, cultures, and societies. By focusing on increasing our social intelligence to guide us in interacting with others, we gradually free ourselves to be meaningful and responsible historical actors who are committed to enriching the common good of all.

When we choose to understand and use our gender potentials according to social intelligence principles, we must acknowledge the strong emotional forces of our sexualities and sexual orientations. We cannot carve out our most meaningful gender choices and gender responsibilities, or seek gender fulfillment, unless we are sufficiently grounded in using our social intelligence to create constructive gender identities, sexualities, and sexual orientations. The principles of social intelligence guide us by continuing to shed light on the power and complexities of history, as well as our personal lives. This means that we not only increase meaning in how we conduct ourselves, but also see the necessary parts we play in creating histories that produce more viable present and future societies for individuals and special interest groups.

XII. History and Gender

Social intelligence not only opens up our lives to scrutiny and new possibilities, but also makes societies more versatile in their evolutionary adaptations to globalization. For example, we benefit from choosing values that make our lives meaningful, and at the same time create a comprehensive common good which is accessible to populations as well as individuals. A universal, wide-ranging common good gradually moves toward social justice, which serves as a purposeful lifetime goal for each one of us and our societies. Therefore, social intelligence encourages us to express our preferred optimal potentials as gendered historical actors, who create their own destinies and futures for societies today and tomorrow.

Gender Defined

We cannot understand what gender means unless we see ourselves and our genders in historical contexts, and know that we are makers of history through our gendered decisions and commitments. For example, social history is a relatively new academic discipline, which highlights the social and intellectual significance of major social influences such as social classes and genders through time. Similarly sociologists, anthropologists, and political scientists have emphasized the significance of families, beliefs, cultures, and societies in human history. Thus, although we always need to take into account physiological aspects of human nature, we must pay attention to the importance of those social characteristics of human behavior that create conditions and environments that compel particular individual and social outcomes.

History is not merely something to be observed, but rather complex social processes that demand and require our participation. Even though each person is at least a passive participant in history, to the extent that we create meaning in our lives we can yearn and aim to accomplish goals that further particular aspects of social progress and civilization. For example, we may teach our children not only to protect themselves, but also to assume responsibilities for those who are less fortunate than they are, as well as for future societies. We need to be thoughtful historical actors, which includes being responsible for our genders, if we are to meet existential imperatives to live fully and increase resources and opportunities for all.

History is particularly useful in guiding us to define genders. We are more objective about our present gendered circumstances, for example, when we know sufficient social facts about past times to reliably compare and contrast patterns of behavior around genders. We see how social classes were and are formed on gender bases, so that generations of women and men were and are still pressured to accept double standards of expectations for women and men. Characteristic patterns of behavior for women and men contrast in basic ways, such as the extent to which each gender is expected to be passive or active. These are crucial aspects of how genders have defined human destinies until fairly recently.

Gender definitions are accepted by individuals and populations in part due to the force of habit when we are young. Our first impressions of who men and women are, and what their lives are like, make strong impacts on how we define genders both when we are young and when we become adults. Unless we use social intelligence to neutralize some of the negative impacts of gender socialization, we may be victims of the power and complexities of conventional gender social influences.

It is imperative that both women and men define their genders carefully. We cannot take genders for granted, or passively accept traditional definitions of gender, if we are to be socially intelligent in our decisions, value choices, and orientations to the common good. Even though our emotional interdependence often suggests that we can lean on traditional ways of doing things, rather than think through the consequences of our actions independently, we must stay committed to being sufficiently awake in our lives that we choose meaningful and challenging paths, which may eventually increase the common good and social justice.

Social intelligence reduces our often-automatic tendencies to use traditional models of gender behavior to guide us. For example, social intelligence principles require us to examine gender definitions in our families, beliefs, social classes, cultures, and societies, in order to be more objective about our genders. Consequently, we increase our gender choices, and proceed to define our genders, so that we are motivated to achieve our preferred goals. In these respects, we are not used or abused by our gender definitions, as much as we are freed through our genders, which helps us to accomplish our most challenging social justice goals.

Gender definitions and gender identities are vital influences on our behavior, because our actions flow from who we think and believe we are as historical beings. When we understand genders in historical contexts we strengthen our knowledge of history, as well as of how gender definitions and gender identities emerge from complex historical influences. Further, we take charge of our destinies and accomplish better futures, when we recognize mistakes of the past sufficiently to create more freedom in defining our present genders.

Gender and Sexuality

History influences our understanding of sexualities, as well as our knowledge of genders. Even though we often fondly imagine that our narrow definitions of human nature will remain unchanged throughout history, when we examine historical trends in sexualities we discover wide ranges of sexual emphases and styles from century to century, and decade to decade. Although these social facts may confound us about the real nature of human nature, social intelligence opens new doors to thinking differently—and more constructively—about genders and sexualities.

A history of sexualities suggests that sexualities are strongly influenced by social conditions such as war or peace, political regimes, social classes, religions, and education. These historical facts show us that our sexualities are not static attributes of human nature, but rather that our sexualities are malleable and respond to changing social circumstances through varied adaptations. Facts about different sexual responses also suggest that we can resolve some of our social contradictions and conflicts about sexualities, by deliberately initiating changes that support and honor sexual diversity.

One of the ways in which sexualities change in different social conditions is the extent to which they are expressed openly. For example, when strong cultural taboos exist, about being homosexual rather than heterosexual, much homosexual sexuality is reactively hidden from public view, with the result that when people are thought to be homosexual they are shunned. Furthermore, even when sexual diversity is widely recognized as a fact of human nature, populations may vary in how effectively they adapt to or welcome this social reality. For example, secretive homosexual cultures continue to develop alongside what were well-established social and legal taboos, so that traditional prejudices and discrimination about homosexual practices often persist.

Social intelligence helps us to recognize and understand how complex and powerful trends in sexualities develop, and what the historical roots are of modern societies' prejudices and discrimination about sexualities. Because genders are closely related to sexualities, no one should ignore these historical facts, or the social realities of sexual diversity. We are only responsible historical actors in relation to our genders and sexualities, when we make commitments to work toward a common good that benefits all, through bringing social justice principles to bear on difficult social situations related to genders and sexualities.

Social intelligence clears our conventional thinking about genders and sexualities, because it requires us to apply societal perspectives to understanding genders and sexualities throughout history. For example, history gives us factual bases for assessing gender diversity and collecting social facts about genders and sexualities. Knowing facts about sexual diversity, sexual prejudices, and sexual discrimination becomes a substantive foundation for initiating social changes to increase opportunities for all through the common good and social justice.

Collecting social facts enables us to define and scrutinize social realities. For example, social facts help us to persuade others that knowing specific truths about sexual diversities reduces public ignorance about the nature of human nature. Furthermore, understanding the flexibility of human adaptations through time yields more productive historical opportunities to do things differently in our present and future societies.

Sexualities are influenced by our gender definitions, as well as by the social facts of sexual diversity. For example, we control our sexualities more when we take charge of our gender definitions and gender identities. Examining our deepest beliefs about our genders, as well as our prejudices and discrimination about sexualities, gradually reduces contradictions and conflicts in our thinking and behavior.

When we clarify destructive aspects of conventional thinking about sexualities that we absorbed through our families, education, religions, social classes, cultures, and societies, we are more likely to let go of ideas that have negative social consequences for all of us. Accepting this daunting challenge is often what it takes to be socially intelligent, responsible historical actors, in terms of our genders and sexualities.

None of our steps to become more aware and more responsible about our genders and sexualities are easy to take, or necessarily well-received by others. However, when we persist in expressing our sexualities through social intelligence principles, we find that our lives are more meaningful, have a clearer sense of purpose, and move in constructive directions for us, our communities, our societies, and our civilizations. For example, we participate more actively in globalization when we see connections among genders, sexualities, and social injustices, as well as commit ourselves to increase the common good in problematic social conditions.

Gender and Sexual Orientation

Although our sexualities are more than our sexual orientations, our sexual orientations are critical in how we establish gender definitions, gender identities, and private or public aspects of sexual behavior. Just as we deepen our knowledge of sexualities, by understanding histories of sexualities in different societies, we deepen our appreciation of the power and complexities of sexual orientations and genders through comparing historical facts. We use history to become more objective about genders, sexualities, and sexual orientations, so that our social intelligence will guide our interpretations of these significant social realities more effectively.

We realize more of the social significance of genders when we trace historical dimensions of sexualities and sexual orientations in societies, and question the extent to which our physiologies are governed by crucial environmental influences, such as emotional interdependence and the effects of families, beliefs, social classes, cultures, and societies on how we think and act. However, to the extent that our relatives do not have contrasting sexual orientations, we may not experience directly the impacts that social and cultural taboos have on sexual orientations in families and societies. Nevertheless, we need to know that many families intensely resist and reject family members who have minority sexual orientations, sometimes excluding their homosexual relatives from family communications and events.

Whether or not family dramas are fought out along lines of contrasting sexual orientations, families are frequently crucibles of prejudices and discrimination about minority sexual orientations. We usually learn—and therefore can unlearn—what sexual bigotry and intolerance are through our families. For example, we can fairly accurately assess the power of our families' biases when we make changes in our own behavior and views about homosexuality or bisexuality. These issues predictably trigger chain reactions from relatives, who then pressure us to go back to our former family ways of thinking and acting. However, because families are common breeding grounds of resistance to sexual diversity, we benefit from taking opportunities to increase our social intelligence about genders and sexual orientations in our families and beyond.

For example, we also increase our social intelligence by considering histories of sexual orientation prejudices and discrimination in communities and societies. This allows us to align ourselves more closely with progressive gender beliefs which embrace sexual diversity. Because beliefs are complex and powerful social influences, we strengthen our social intelligence by focusing on the social origins of our own beliefs, which may include interactions with relatives, teachers, politicians, or community leaders.

Becoming more objective about our destructive and constructive beliefs on sexual orientations increases our social intelligence, so that we make wiser value choices. For example, deciding to nurture values such as equality, inclusiveness, diversity, cooperation, and openness moves us closer to reducing our prejudices and discrimination about sexual orientations, so that we gradually accept and embrace differences in sexual orientations.

People who are explicit about their minority sexual orientations are frequently considered to be in lower social classes than those with majority sexual orientations. In these respects, heterosexual values and priorities are usually reflected in higher social class life chances than homosexual, bisexual, or transsexual values and priorities. However, when we understand that homosexual, bisexual, and transsexual orientations are gendered social classes, we are better equipped to break out of any ostracized isolation, because we see that our restricted opportunities and options are closely tied to those who have similar sexual orientations. Historically, social movements for minority sexual orientation rights often begin with socially intelligent awareness of gendered and sexually oriented social class divisions.

One reason that attitudes about sexual orientations are deep-seated is that sexual orientation values derive from both mainstream and special interest cultures. For example, we absorb gender values from family and community cultures that have supported or rejected particular sexual orientations. Thus, historical cultural values either limit or free individuals and groups with different sexual orientations, whereas social intelligence guides us to make new value choices that have constructive gendered or sexual orientation purposes and directions for all in the present for the future. Social intelligence motivates us to increase the common good and social justice now, according to cultural value choices such as equality, inclusiveness, diversity, cooperation, and openness.

Although social intelligence and history help us to explore genders and sexual orientations in families, beliefs, social classes, cultures, and societies, applying the broadest context of societies in our thinking and acting is particularly important. For example, when we consider genders and sexual orientations from the points of view of histories of individual societies, civilizations, and globalization, we understand more fully what drives world changes and resistance to changes about sexual orientations. We are also more likely to commit ourselves to being historical actors who educate us all about genders and sexual orientations, in order to banish ignorance and make wiser gender choices. When we are successful in these endeavors, we use social intelligence to create better futures for all genders and sexual orientations.

Gender Choices

History reveals shifts in gender awareness and gender choices throughout the ages, which in part depend on how publics understand their gender options. The development of democracies multiplied definitions of individual and social rights, so that making choices increasingly became a way of life in modern societies. Gone are strong public beliefs in fate, where superior powers—religious or political—are not challenged. In their place are beliefs in secular forces such as science and technology, where human beings have goals that may counter the rule of despots or tyrannical mobs. Laws have become increasingly important during modern times, and gender choices have moved from accepting the status quo to creating new individual and social gender identities.

Even sketchy broad historical perspectives give us hope that social conditions for genders, sexualities, and sexual orientations are improving, and that recent generations have benefitted from increased gender choices. We not only see our own genders differently as women and men, but make new assumptions about human capacities to move in directions which expand the common good and social justice. For example the entrapment in social classes, that early twentieth century populations tolerated or even encouraged, is no longer accepted in many modern twenty-first century societies. We know that we have more choices today—including variations in genders, sexualities, and sexual orientations—so that we are continuously motivated to achieve our preferred goals rather than traditional objectives.

Social intelligence suggests that histories of families, beliefs, social classes, cultures, and societies are significant ways to understand the origins and depths of our current gender choices. When we understand how our choices evolved, for example, we are more likely to pay close attention to our options today, so that we do not lose opportunities or accomplishments that help us to achieve our preferred goals. Knowing what our priorities are now, as well as being sufficiently free to pursue them, helps us to go forward effectively with increased meaning and purpose in our everyday lives.

To some extent we think that the choices we make about our families and beliefs are private matters that do not have significant impacts on others. However, social intelligence emphasizes that because we are emotionally interdependent beings, we need to pay particular attention to how we and other family members maintain patterns of dependency in our closest relationships, which influence our beliefs and how we think. Thus, families and beliefs are foundations of our being and acting in the world.

Social intelligence not only points out the strong negative effects of these inhibiting family and belief influences, but also shows us that increasing our objectivity creates ways out of being immobilized by others' expectations. At the same time that we detach from family pressures, for example, we see alternative choices and pursue them more fully. Consequently, we are more likely to be sufficiently independent to let go of contradictory beliefs, so that we more actively choose to nurture beliefs that inspire us to accomplish our chosen goals.

Our choices about social classes, cultures, and societies often seem to be more superficial, and therefore less likely to impact the quality of our lives, than our choices about families and beliefs. However, the perspectives of social classes, cultures, and societies are vital, necessary influences in their own right, which critically affect how we experience our genders, sexualities, and sexual orientations. Thus, we need to understand patterns of historical changes in social classes, cultures, and societies if we are to increase our choices in genders, sexualities, and sexual orientations today. For example, clarifying our ongoing meanings, purposes, and directions enables us to build more progressive societies with freer gender, sexuality, and sexual orientation choices.

Social intelligence emphasizes the importance of making new value choices when we want to be guided by social intelligence principles. For example, we are more likely to change problematic aspects of our genders, sexualities, and sexual orientations when we focus on choosing constructive social values such as equality, inclusiveness, diversity, cooperation, and openness. These values prepare individuals and groups to pursue the common good and social justice successfully. They also nurture supportive social conditions which increase life chances, opportunities, and choices for people of all genders, sexualities, and sexual orientations. Thus, our value choices as gendered beings are effective ways to usher in new values that create meaningful, productive contemporary and future societies.

Gender Responsibilities

Social intelligence increases our awareness of the importance and social significance of being more responsible historical actors. History is vital not only to help us to understand why social intelligence is such a rich source of meanings, but also to see why being responsible, active participants in history is rewarding and beneficial to all. For example, we cannot express our genders, sexualities, and sexual orientations fully, without first considering how gendered definitions and choices have changed through time, having varied impacts on our responsibilities.

Social intelligence requires us to apply historical approaches to understanding who we are in relation to families, beliefs, social classes, cultures, and societies. When we focus on questioning what our gender responsibilities are in families, beliefs, social classes, cultures, and societies, we find some possible answers through reviewing historical information. For example, comparisons of gender responsibilities, that members of different societies assume, show us not only contrasting power dimensions such as democracies and autocracies, but also contrasts in qualities of social conditions and everyday experiences.

Historical information about different families is particularly illuminating when it spells out nuances and details about social expectations for men and women throughout their lives. We compare different attitudes in different epochs, which deepens our understanding of double standards in gender expectations and gender responsibilities, even in contemporary societies. These social facts show us that we can change our commitments today, because trends in gender responsibilities are socially learned. Furthermore, we need to be cautious in assuming gender responsibilities, because social commitments necessarily define our life outcomes.

Some of the nuts and bolts of the gender responsibilities we accept, and the gender commitments we make, are found in histories of our personal and social beliefs. For example, when we know to what extent gendered social attitudes have been upheld through time, we realize the continuing depth of contemporary issues around gender in modern societies. Social controls over defining gender responsibilities were not put into place recently, and people with vested interests are reluctant to let go of traditions in attitudes and behavior that continue to restrict or promote specific genders, sexualities, and sexual orientations. Using history to increase our objectivity about gender responsibilities ultimately frees us to be more mature in our choices about how and why we make individual and social gender commitments.

Being objective about our social classes, especially our gendered social classes, gives us more freedom of choice to make deeper commitments. When we are socially intelligent, we do not automatically accept traditional social class values and attitudes, but rather question what it is that we really want to do with our lives in terms of gendered social classes. Witnessing changes in social class responsibilities through history gives us broader and deeper senses of which gendered social facts are most compelling in our societies, and how we can loosen the hold of social class dominance in defining what our gender responsibilities are today for tomorrow.

Inspiration about gender responsibilities is also found in rich cultural sources of information. Histories of knowledge, education, sciences, arts, legal systems, and religions highlight significant aspects of cultures and civilizations that can lead us in new directions for practicing social intelligence principles. We become who we are in large part because of our earliest value choices, but we can also change who we are and how we define our responsibilities through making new value choices in our cultures.

Historical facts show us that our ongoing gender responsibilities and commitments look different when we make value choices which support equality, inclusiveness, diversity, cooperation, and openness. These social justice values guide us to express the common good in ways that enhance the genders, sexualities, and sexual orientations of all, rather than the well-being of members of powerful social classes and their cultures.

Lastly, and perhaps most important, we are beholden to how societies describe and explain history and gender responsibilities. Sometimes national descriptions and explanations are articulated in laws, traditions, and civic histories. For example, we develop powerful gendered world views through patriotic values, although this inevitably also biases or narrows some of our value choices and gender responsibilities.

Social intelligence shows us how historical necessities continue to create national and international world views of gender, and at the same time requires us to question whether these can be productive in a socially just world. Our socially intelligent goal is to welcome globalization, and create social conditions that promote cooperative gender responsibilities to solve world problems, which include intransigent issues about genders, sexualities, and sexual orientations.

XII. History and Gender

Gender Fulfillment

Although social intelligence is primarily concerned with establishing social conditions for the survival and fulfillment of all members of societies and civilizations, we need to examine gender fulfillment closely if these goals are to be met. Because genders and sexualities are vital components of human nature, we have to honor real gender needs in order to live in the most viable conditions of equality, inclusiveness, diversity, cooperation, and openness.

Gender identity and our definitions of gender not only govern how we spend our lives, but also whether or not we attain a satisfying degree of individual and social gender fulfillment. For example, social intelligence assesses which human needs should be recognized in optimal social conditions, as well as how we can go about meeting both survival and fulfillment needs. Although survival needs are more imperative than fulfillment needs, we cannot live fully unless we use our potentials to respond to others' needs as well as our own.

Gender fulfillment is central in our endeavors to live meaningfully, because genders are at the core of our freedoms as individuals, human beings, and historical actors. When we organize our lives around socially intelligent priorities, we must focus on genders and gender fulfillment, so that we do not lose energies and interests to build a practical common good and social justice. Ideally, our gendered beings and gendered actions move us to choose life-enhancing priorities, which create the real hope we offer for better worlds.

Our genders, sexualities, and sexual orientations need to be expressed with social intelligence if we are to make wise decisions and strategic choices in being responsible historical actors who increase gender fulfillment. For example, social intelligence encourages us to think through how to deal effectively with challenging gender situations. We cannot hide from these demands, because we want to live fully rather than insulate ourselves from complex gender influences. In this context, social intelligence helps us to gain some control over our gendered priorities, goals, and outcomes.

When we pay sufficient attention to history—which includes what is happening in the present as well as what has already happened—we increase our clarity about how to intervene in the five major social influences of families, beliefs, social classes, cultures, and societies. For example, social intelligence not only establishes these priorities, but gives us more objective views of our situations, so that we identify gender options and gender responsibilities in rapidly changing social conditions more easily and more accurately.

Maintaining objectivity throughout our efforts to increase the common good minimizes our gender and sexual biases, as well as prepares us to move in directions which improve genders and social conditions. Heading in these directions, rather than solely trying to achieve personal idealistic goals, brings us gender fulfillment and satisfaction as whole human beings. Although we need to believe that we can accomplish our gendered objectives, we also have to be pragmatic and realistic in making constructive adaptations to difficult issues related to genders, sexualities, and sexual orientations.

Furthermore, we choose to believe that all our efforts to achieve gender changes count and are needed. Even though we may be unwilling to assume particular gendered responsibilities, our actions still influence outcomes, ideals, and fulfillment. At best, this means that we will not be deterred from aspiring to what may seem to be impossible objectives at present, because history shows us that our futures depend on what we believe and do now. In these respects, social intelligence creates new gender beginnings which do not merely repeat mistakes of the past.

Thus, our starting points in gaining gender fulfillment are not only a beginning, but a resource to be returned to at any stage of our lifetime journeys. We remember, for example, that we are emotionally interdependent human beings, who need to be inspired by our cultures as well as supported in our flawed efforts to reach our well-intentioned goals. When we persist in cultivating awareness of the five major social influences of families, beliefs, social classes, cultures, and societies through our actions, we live

XII. History and Gender

at the heart of social intelligence. Consequently, living each day according to principles of social intelligence enlightens, guides, and secures our individual and social gender fulfillment. And these are just some of the indescribably meaningful benefits of using social intelligence to enliven our genders and bring about improved futures for all.

Suggested Reading

Altman, Dennis. 2001. *Global Sex*. Chicago IL: University of Chicago Press.

Andersen, Margaret. 2003. *Thinking About Women: Sociological Perspectives on Sex and Gender*, 6th edition. Boston, MA: Allyn and Bacon.

Brownmiller, Susan. 1999. *In Our Time: Memoir of a Revolution*. New York: Dial Press.

Butler, Judith. 1999. *Gender Trouble: Feminism and the Subversion of Identity*. Berkeley, CA: University of California Press.

Chesler, Phyllis. 2001. *Woman's Inhumanity to Woman*. New York: Nation's Books.

Collins, Patricia Hill. 2000. *Black Feminist Thought: Knowledge, Consciousness, and Empowerment*, 2nd ed. New York: Routledge.

Collins, Patricia Hill. 2004. *Black Sexual Politics: African Americans, Gender, and the New Racism*. New York: Routledge.

Connell, R. W. 1995. *Masculinities*. Berkeley, CA: University of California Press.

Craig, Maxine Leeds. 2002. *Ain't I a Beauty Queen? Black Women, Beauty, and the Politics of Race*. New York: Oxford University Press.

Davis, Angela. 1989. *Women, Culture, and Politics*. New York: Random House.

Dickinson, Torry D., and Robert K. Schaeffer, eds. 2008. *Transformations: Feminist Pathways to Global Change: An Analytical Anthology*. Boulder, CO: Paradigm.

Enloe, Cynthia. 1989. *Bananas, Beaches, and Bases: Making Feminist Sense of International Politics*. London: Pandora Press.

Espiritu, Yen Le. 1996. *Asian American Women and Men*. Thousand Oaks, CA: Sage. Publishers.

Freedman, Estelle B., and John D'Emilio. 1988. *Intimate Matters: A History of Sexuality in America*. New York: Routledge.

Freedman, Estelle B. 2002. *No Turning Back: The History of Feminism and the Future of Women*. New York: Ballantine.

Fujiwara, Lynn. 2008. *Mothers without Citizenship: Asian Immigrant Families and the Consequences of Welfare Reform*. Minneapolis, MN: University of Minnesota Press.

Hurtado, Aida. 2003. *Voicing Chicano Feminisms: Young Women Speak Out on Sexuality and Identity.* New York: New York University Press.

Irvine, Janice M. 2002. *Talk about Sex: The Battles over Sex Education in the United States.* Berkeley, CA: University of California Press.

Kimmel, Michael S. 1996. *Manhood in America: A Cultural History.* New York: The Free Press.

Kimmel, Michael S., and Michael A. Messner. 2000. *Men's Lives,* 5th ed. Needham Heights, MA: Allyn and Bacon.

Nardi, Peter M., and Beth Schneider. 1997. *Social Perspectives on Lesbian and Gay Studies.* New York: Routledge.

Roberts, Dorothy. 1997. *Killing the Black Body: Race, Reproduction and the Meaning of Liberty.* New York: Vintage Books.

Schwartz, Pepper, and Virginia Rutter. 1998. *The Gender of Sexuality.* Thousand Oaks, CA: Pine Forge Press.

With many thanks to my colleagues at Georgetown University Sociology Department, the Bowen Center for the Study of the Family, the Association for Applied and Clinical Sociology, and the International Sociological Association (Research Committee 46, Clinical Sociology). I am also indebted to my clients and students, who have taught me so much, and to my wonderful American and English families, who continue to stand by me on a daily basis.

www.ingramcontent.com/pod-product-compliance
Lightning Source LLC
Chambersburg PA
CBHW030432290526
45786CB00001B/260